THE PARTHIAN PERIOD

INSTITUTE OF RELIGIOUS ICONOGRAPHY
STATE UNIVERSITY GRONINGEN

ICONOGRAPHY OF RELIGIONS

EDITED BY

Th. P. van Baaren, L. P. van den Bosch, H. G. Kippenberg, L. Leertouwer
F. Leemhuis, H. te Velde, H. Witte, and H. Buning (*Secretary*)

SECTION XIV: IRAN

FASCICLE THREE

LEIDEN
E. J. BRILL
1986

THE PARTHIAN PERIOD

BY

MALCOLM A. R. COLLEDGE

With 48 plates

LEIDEN

E. J. BRILL

1986

ISBN 90 04 07115 6

PRINTED IN THE NETHERLANDS BY E. J. BRILL

CONTENTS

ACKNOWLEDGEMENTS

It is a pleasure to acknowledge the generous assistance received from a great number of individuals and institutions over the past twenty years. The British Academy provided a grant for travel, and the British Schools of Archaeology in Iran and Iraq gave valuable aid and hospitality. The Directors and staff of the Archaeological Services and Museums of Iran, Afghanistan, Pakistan, India, Iraq, Syria, Lebanon and Turkey have been extremely generous with permissions to study material and to reproduce items as illustrations. The Institut français d'archéologie in Beirut, the Délégation archéologique française en Afghanistan and Yale University Art Gallery have been equally kind. Many individuals have also been generous with their time and with permissions, including Dr. A. D. H. Bivar, Mrs. C. M. Bradford, Dr. J. J. Coulton, Anna Czerniawska, Dr. F. K. Dörner, Professor S. B. Downey, Dr. M. Gawlikowski, the late Professor R. Ghirshman, Madame T. Ghirshman, Dr. J. Hansman, Dr. J. G. F. Hind, Mr. Jabir Ibrahim, Professor H. Ingholt, Professor G. A. Pugachenkova, Samira Salbi, Professor J. B. Segal, the late Henri Seyrig and Professor L. Vanden Berghe.

Without such help this monograph could not have been written at all; its deficiencies are the responsibility of the author.

MALCOLM A. R. COLLEDGE

SELECT BIBLIOGRAPHY

Abbreviations

AA — *Jahrbuch des deutschen archäologischen Instituts, Archäologische Anzeiger*, Berlin

AAS — *Annales archéologiques de Syrie*

AJA — *American Journal of Archaeology*

AL-SALIHI, Sculptures — AL-SALIHI, W., *The sculptures of divinities from Hatra*, (Doctoral Dissertation) Princeton University 1969

AMI (n.f.) — *Archäologische Mitteilungen aus Iran (neue Folge)*

AS — SEYRIG, H., *Antiquités Syriennes* I-VI, Paris 1934-1966

BSOAS — *Bulletin of the School of Oriental and African Studies*, London

CIS — *Corpus Inscriptionum Semiticarum*

COLLEDGE, Palmyra — COLLEDGE, M. A. R., The art of Palmyra, London 1976

COLLEDGE, Parthian art — COLLEDGE, M. A. R., *Parthian art*, London 1977

CRAI — *Comptes Rendus de l'Académie des Inscriptions et belles-lettres*, Paris

DAFA — *Délégation archéologique française en Afghanistan*

Dir. Ant., Baghdad — Directorate General of Antiquities, Baghdad

DRIJVERS, Religion — DRIJVERS, H. J. W., "The religion of Palmyra", *Iconography of Religions* XV, 15, Leiden 1976

Dura Prelim. Rep. — scc below, s.v. ROSTOVTZEFF, M. I.

Dura Final Rep. — see below, s.v. BELLINGER, A. R.

GHIRSHMAN, Iran — GHIRSHMAN, R., *Iran, Parthians and Sassanians*, London 1962

Ht. — Hatra, site number

HUMANN, Reisen — HUMANN, C., and PUCHSTEIN, O., *Reisen in Kleinasien und Nordsyrien*, Berlin 1890

InfA — Institut français d'archéologie, Beirut

IUTAKE — (*Trudi*) *Iujno-Turkmenistanskoi Arkheologitcheskoi Komplexnoi Expeditsii*, Ashkhabad and Moscow

JNES — *Journal of Near Eastern Studies*

JRAS — *Journal of the Royal Asiatic Society*

MDAI — *Mémoires de la délégation archéologique en Iran*, Paris

SAFAR, Hatra — SAFAR, F. and MUSTAFA, M. A., *Hatra: the city of the Sun God* (in Arabic), Baghdad 1974

SCHLUMBERGER, Palmyrène — SCHLUMBERGER, D., *La Palmyrène du nord-ouest*, Paris 1951

VDI — *Vestnik Drevnei Istorii*, Moscow

WALDMANN, Kultref. — WALDMANN, H., *Die kommagenischen Kultreformen unter König Mithradates I und seinen Sohne Antiochos I*, Leiden 1973

WVDOG — *Wissenschaftliche Veröffentlichungen der deutschen Orient-Gesellschaft*, Leipzig

Select Bibliography

ABGARIANS, M. T. and SELLWOOD, D. G., "A hoard of early Parthian drachms", *Numismatic Chronicle* (7th series) 11, 1971, 103-119.

AL-SALIHI, W., *The sculptures of divinities from Hatra*, (Doctoral Dissertation) Princeton University, 1969.

——, "Hatra, aspects of Hatran religion", *Sumer* 26, 1970, 187-194.

——, "Hercules-Nergal at Hatra (II)", *Iraq* 35, 1973, 65-68.

AMIET, P. and STRONACH, D., *Suse. Site et musée*, Teheran 1973.

ANDRAE, W., "Hatra", I, *WVDOG* 9, 1908; II, *WVDOG* 21, 1912.
ANDRAE, W. and LENZEN, H., "Die Partherstadt Assur", *WVDOG* 57, 1933.
ANDRAE, W., *Das wiedererstehende Assur*, Leipzig 1938.
BELENITSKY, A., *Central Asia*, London 1969.
BELLINGER, A. R. and others (eds.), *The excavations at Dura-Europos. Final Report*, vols. I-VIII, New Haven, New York and Los Angeles 1943 -.
BERNARD, P., *Fouilles d'Aï Khanoum*, I, II, Paris 1973.
——, "Les traditions orientales dans l'architecture gréco-bactrienne", *Journal Asiatique* 264, 1976, 245-275.
BIEBER, M., *The sculpture of the Hellenistic age*, revised edition New York 1961.
BIVAR A. D. H. and SHAKED, S., "The inscriptions at Shimbar", *BSOAS* 27, 1964, 265-290.
BIVAR, A. D. H., "Mithra and Mesopotamia", in: HINNELS, J. R., ed., *Mithraic studies*, Manchester 1975, II, 275-289.
——, "Mithraic images of Bactria: are they related to Roman Mithraism?" in: *Mysteria Mithrae, Études préliminaires aux religions orientales dans l'empire romain* 80, Leiden 1979, 743-750.
BOETHIUS, A. and WARD PERKINS, J. B., *Etruscan and Roman architecture*, London 1970.
BORKOWSKA, T., "Palmyreńskie reliefy wotywne (Les bas-reliefs votifs de Palmyre)", *Studia Palmyreńskie* 1, 1966, 96-125.
BOSSERT, H. T., *Altsyrien*, Tübingen 1951.
BOUNNI, A., "Nouveaux bas-reliefs religieux de la Palmyrène", in *Mélanges K. Michalowski*, Warsaw 1966, 313-320.
BOYCE, M., "A history of Zoroastrianism", in: *Handbuch der Orientalistik* VIII, I-IV, Leiden 1975 -.
BRYKCZYŃSKI, P., "Astrologia w Palmyrze", *Studia Palmyreńskie* 7, 1975, 47-109.
DU BUISSON, R. DU MESNIL, *Tessères et monnaies de Palmyre*, I, II, Paris 1944, 1962.
——, "Première campagne de fouilles à Palmyre", *CRAI* 1966, 158-190.
CAMBRIDGE HISTORY OF IRAN, III (1) and (2), ed. E. Yarshater, *The Seleucid, Parthian and Sasanian periods*, Cambridge, 1983.
CANTINEAU, J., *Inventaire des inscriptions de Palmyre*, I-IX, Beirut 1930-1933.
CAQUOT, A., "Chadrapha à propos de quelques articles récents", *Syria* 29, 1952, 74-88.
——, "Note sur le sémeion et les inscriptions araméennes de Hatra", *Syria* 32, 1955, 59-69.
——, "Sur l'onomastique religieuse de Palmyre", *Syria* 39, 1962, 231-256.
CHABOT, J. B. and others, eds., *Répertoire d'épigraphie sémitique*, Paris.
——, *Choix d'inscriptions de Palmyre*, Paris 1922.
CHAUMONT, M. L., "Le culte d'Anâhitâ à Stakhr", *Revue de l'histoire des religions*, 1958, 154-175.
CHRISTIDES, V., *Greek goddesses in the Near East*, New York 1977.
COLLART, P. and VICARI, J., *Le sanctuaire de Baalshamin à Palmyre*, I, II, Rome 1969.
COLLEDGE, M. A. R., *The Parthians*, London 1967.
——, *The art of Palmyra*, London 1976.
——, *Parthian art*, London 1977.
COLLIMET GUÉRIN, P., *Histoire du nimbe des origines au temps modernes*, Paris 1961.
CORPUS INSCRIPTIONUM IRANICARUM, ed. HENNING, W. B., I-V, London 1955-1957.
——, Supplementary Series, ed. GIGNOUX, P., I, London 1972.
CORPUS INSCRIPTIONUM SEMITICARUM, II, Paris 1926-1947.
CUMONT, F., *After-life in Roman paganism*, New Haven 1922.
——, *Fouilles de Doura-Europos*, Paris 1926.
——, *Recherches sur le symbolisme funéraire des romains*, Paris 1942.
——, *The mysteries of Mithra*, London 1956.
DAREMBERG, C., SAGLIO, E. and POTTIER, W., *Dictionnaire des antiquités grecques et romaines*, Paris 1877-1919.
DAWKINS, A. and WOOD, R., *Les ruines de Palmyre*, London and Paris 1753.
DEBEVOISE, N. C., *A political history of Parthia*, Chicago 1938.
——, "Rock reliefs of ancient Iran", *JNES* 1, 1942, 76-105.
DEHEJIA, V., *Early Buddhist rock temples*, London 1972.
DENTZER, J. M., "Reliefs au banquet dans la moitié orientale de l'empire romain: iconographie hellénistique et traditions locales", *Revue archéologique* 1978, 63-82.
DIAKONOV, I. M. and LIVSHITS, V. A., *Dokumenty iz Nisy*, Moscow 1960.
DÖRNER, F. K., "Arsameia am Nymphaios", *AA* 1965, 188-235.
——, "Zur Rekonstruktion der Ahnengalerie des Königs Antiochos I. von Kommagene", *Istanbuler Mitteilungen* 17, 1967, 195-210.
DOWNEY, S. B., "Cult banks from Hatra", *Berytus* 16, 1966, 97-109.
——, "The Heracles sculpture", *The excavations at Dura-Europos, Final Report* III, I, 1, New York 1969.
——, "A preliminary corpus of the Standards of Hatra", *Sumer* 26, 1970, 195-226.

DOWNEY, S. B., " 'Temples à escaliers': the Dura evidence", *California Studies in Classical Antiquity* 9, 1976, 21-39.

——, "The stone and plaster sculpture", *The excavations at Dura-Europos, Final Report* III, I, 2, Los Angeles 1977.

DRIJVERS, H. J. W., "The religion of Palmyra", *Iconography of Religions* XV, 15, Leiden 1976.

——, "Hatra, Palmyra und Edessa", in: TEMPORINI, H. and HAASE, W., *Aufstieg und Niedergang der römischen Welt*, II, 8, Tübingen 1977, 799-906.

——, "Mithra at Hatra?", *Acta Iranica* 4, 1978, 151-186.

——, "Cults and beliefs at Edessa", *Études préliminaires aux religions orientales dans l'empire romain* 82, Leiden 1980.

DUCHESNE-GUILLEMAN, J., *Religion de l'Iran ancien*, Paris 1962.

DUNANT, C., "Nouvelles tessères de Palmyre", *Syria* 36, 1959, 102-110.

——, "Les inscriptions", *Le sanctuaire de Baalshamin à Palmyre*, III, Rome 1971.

EDDY, S. K., *The king is dead: Studies in the Near Eastern resistance to Hellenism, 334-31B.C.* Nebraska 1961.

EISSFELDT, C., *Tempel und Kulte syrischer Städte in hellenistisch-römischer Zeit*, Leipzig 1941.

ERDMANN, K, "Das iranische Feierheiligtum", *Sendschriften der deutsche Orient-Gesellschaft* 11, Leipzig 1941.

FARD, K., "Kangavâr", *Iran* 11, 1973, 190-197.

FARMAKOWSKY, B. V., "Painting in Palmyra" (in Russian), *Bulletin of the Russian archaeological Institute in Constantinople* 8, 1903, 172-198.

FÉVRIER, J. G., *La religion des palmyréniens*, Paris 1932.

FRANKFORT, H., *The art and architecture of the Ancient Orient*, 4th edn., London 1970.

FRÉZOULS, E. (ed.), "Palmyre, bilan et perspectives", *Travaux du centre de recherche sur le proche-orient et la Grèce antiques* 3, Strasbourg 1976.

FRUMKIN, G., *Archaeology in Soviet Central Asia*, Leiden 1970.

FRYE, R, N., *The heritage of Persia*, London 1962.

——, "Mithra in Iranian history", in: HINNELLS, J R (ed.), *Mithraic studies*, I, Manchester 1975, 62-67.

GALL, H. VON, "Die Kulträume in den Felsen von Karaftu bei Takab (West-Azerbaidjan)", *AMI* n f 11, 1978, 91-112.

——, "Ikonographische Quellen zur iranischen Mythologie der parthischen und sasanidischen Periode", in: HAUSSIG, H. W. (ed.), *Wörterbuch der Mythologie* (forthcoming).

GARDNER, P., *The coins of the Greek and Scythic kings of Bactria and India in the British Museum*, London 1886.

GAWLIKOWSKI, M., "Problemy ikonografii kapłanow palmyreńskie", *Studia Palmyreńskie* 1, 1966, 74-96.

——, "Die polnischen Ausgrabungen in Palmyra 1959-1967", *AA* 1968, 289-307.

——, "À propos des reliefs du temple des Gaddê à Doura", *Berytus* 18, 1969, 105-109.

——, "Monuments funéraires de Palmyre", *Travaux du centre d'archéologie mediterranéenne de l'Académie polonaise des sciences* 9, Warsaw 1970.

——, *Le temple palmyrénien*, Warsaw 1973.

——, "Le temple d'Allat à Palmyre", *Revue archéologique* 1977, 253-274.

GOOSSENS, G., *Hiérapolis de Syrie*, Paris 1943.

GHIRSHMAN, R., "La tour de Nourabad", *Syria* 24, 1944-1945, 175-193.

——, *Iran, Parthians and Sassanians*, London 1962.

——, "Terrasses sacrées de Bard-è Néchandeh et de Masjid-i Solaiman", *MDAI* 15, I, II, Paris 1976.

Goodenough, E. R., *Jewish symbols in the Greco-Roman period*, I-XIII, New York and Princeton 1953-1968.

GULLINI, G., *Architettura iranica dagli Achemenidi ai Sasanidi. Il "palazzo" di Kuh-i Khwagia, Seistan*, Turin 1964.

——, "Preliminary report of the excavations at Seleucia and Ctesiphon", *Mesopotamia* 1-9, 1964-1973.

GUTMANN, J. (ed.), *The Dura-Europos Synagogue: a re-evaluation (1932-72)*, Montana 1973.

HACKIN, J., "Recherches archéologiques à Bégram", *Mémoires de la DAFA* 9, 1939; 11, 1954.

HAERINCK, E., "Quelques monuments funéraires de l'île de Kharg dans le golfe persique", *Iranica Antiqua* 11; 1975, 194-67.

HALLADE, M., *Gandharan art of north India*, New York 1968.

HANSMAN, J. and STRONACH, D., "Excavations at Shahr-i Qumis, 1971", *JRAS* 1974, 8-22.

HENNING, W. B., "The monuments and inscriptions of Tang-i Sarvak", *Asia Major* 2, 1952, 151-171.

——, "Mitteliranisch", in: *Handbuch der Orientalistik* I, 4, Leiden 1958.

HERZFELD, E., *Am Tor von Asien*, Berlin 1920.

——, *Archaeological history of Iran*, Oxford 1935.

——, *Iran in the ancient east*, Oxford 1941.

HILL, G. F., *Catalogue of the Greek coins of Arabia, Mesopotamia and Persia in the British Museum*, London 1922.

HOMÈS-FREDERICQ, D., *Hatra et ses sculptures parthes*, Istanbul 1963.

HOPKINS, C., "The Parthian temple", *Berytus* 7, 1942, 1-18.

HOPKINS, C. (ed.), *Topography and architecture of Seleucia on the Tigris*, Ann Arbor, 1972.

HUMANN, K. and PUCHSTEIN, C., *Reisen in Kleinasien und Nordsyrien*, Berlin 1890.

INGHOLT, H., *Studier over Palmyrensk Skulptur*, Copenhagen 1928.

——, "Parthian sculptures from Hatra", *Memoirs of the Connecticut Academy of Arts and Sciences* 12, 1954.

——, *Gandharan art in Pakistan*, New York 1957.

INGHOLT, H., SEYRIG, H. and STARCKY, J., *Recueil des tessères de Palmyre*, Paris 1955.

JEPPESEN, K., "A Hellenistic fortress on the island of Ikaros (Faïlaka) in the Persian Gulf", in: *VIIIe Congrès international d'archéologie classique*, Paris 1965, 541-544.

JORDAN, J. and PREUSSER, C., "Uruk-Warka", *WVDOG* 51, 1928.

KEALL, R. J., "Qalʿeh-i Yazdigird: the question of its date", *Iran* 15, 1977, 1-9.

KHAZAI, K., "L'évolution et la signification du griffon dans l'iconographie iranienne", *Iranica Antiqua* 13, 1978, 1-34.

KIEFFER, C. M., "Kusana art and the historic effigies of Mat (India) and Surkh Kotal (Afghanistan)", *Mârg* 15, (Bombay) March 1962, 43-49.

KLENGEL, H., "Babylon zur Zeit der Perser, Griechen und Parther", *Forschungen und Berichte, Staatliche Museen zu Berlin* 5, Berlin 1962, 40-53.

KOSHELENKO, G. A., *Kultura Parfii*, Moscow 1966.

KRAELING, C. H., "The Synagogue", *The excavations at Dura-Europos, Final Report* VIII, 1, New Haven 1956.

——, "Colour photographs of the paintings in the Tomb of the Three Brothers", *AAS* 11-12, 1961-1962, 13-18.

——, "The Christian Building", *The excavations at Dura-Europos, Final Report*, New Haven 1967.

KRUNIČ, J., "Hatra: l'architecture des temples au centre de la ville: questions relatives à leur construction", *Revue archéologique* 1964, 7-32.

KRZECHOWICZ, G., "Uwagi nad Geneza świątyń Palmyreńskich (Remarks on the origins of Palmyrene temples)", *Studia Palmyreńskie* 5, 1974, 45-82.

LAHIRI, A. N., *Corpus of Indo-Greek coins*, Calcutta 1965.

LENZEN, H., "Ausgrabungen in Hatra", *AA* 1955, 334-375.

——, "Architektur der Partherzeit in Mesopotamien", in: *Festschrift* C. WEICKERT, Berlin 1955, 121-136.

LE RIDER, G., "Suse sous les Séleucides et les Parthes", *MDAI* 38, 1965.

LEROY, J., "Mosaïques funéraires d'Édesse", *Syria* 24, 1957, 306-342.

LEWIS, B. and others (eds.), *The Encyclopedia of Islam*, London 1965 -.

ŁUKASIAK, E., "Ikonografia Yarhibôla", *Studia Palmyreńskie* 5, 1974, 7-44.

LUKONIN, V. G., "The temple of Anahita in Kangavar" (in Russian), *VDI* 1977 (2), 105-111.

MARSHALL, J., *Taxila*, I-III, Cambridge 1951.

——, *A guide to Taxila*, 4th edn., Cambridge 1960.

——, *The Buddhist art of Gandhara*, Cambridge 1960.

MASSON, M. E. and PUGACHENKOVA, G. A., (Nisa reports) *Trudi IUTAKE*, Ashkhabad and Moscow, 1, 1949; 4.1, 1959; 4.2, 1956.

MASSON, M. E., "Nisa Parthica", in: *Enciclopedia dell'Arte Antica* 5, Rome 1965, 533-534.

MATHESON, S. A., *Persia: an archaeological guide*, London 1972.

MICHALOWSKI, K., *Palmyre: Fouiles polonaises 1959, 1960, 1961, 1962, 1963-1964*, Warsaw and Paris 1960-1966.

MILIK, J. T., *Dédicaces faites par des dieux*, Paris 1972.

MITCHINER, M., *Indo-Greek and Indo-Scythian coinage*, I-VI, London 1975.

MONGAIT, A. L., *Archaeology in the U.S.S.R.*, London 1961.

MOREHART, M., "Early sculpture at Palmyra", *Berytus* 12, 1956-1957, 53-83.

NARAIN, A. K., *The Indo-Greeks*, Oxford 1957.

NAUMANN, R., HUFF, D., and SCHNYDER, R., "Takht-i Suleiman. Bericht über die Ausgrabungen 1965-1973", *AA* 1975, 109-204.

NEUSNER, J., *A history of the Jews in Babylonia*, I: the Parthian period, Leiden 1965.

POPE, A. U., *A survey of Persian art*, I-VI, Oxford 1938.

PUGACHENKOVA, G. A., "Puty razvitija arkhitektury iužnogo Turkmenistana pory rabovladenija i feodalizma", *Trudi IUTAKE* 6, Moscow 1958.

——, "Margianskaya boginia", *Sovietskaya Arkheologiya* 29-30, 1959, 119-140.

——, *Iskusstvo Turkmenistana*, Moscow 1967.

——, *Skulptura Khalčajana*, Moscow 1971.

——, "Archaeological light on Bactrian cults" (in Russian), *VDI* 1974 (3), 124-135.

RICHTER, G. M. A., "Ancient plaster casts of Greek metalware", *AJA* 62, 1958, 369-377.

ROSENFIELD, J. M., *The dynastic arts of the Kushans*, Los Angeles 1967.

ROSTOVTZEFF, M. I. and others (eds.), *The excavations at Dura-Europos. Preliminary Reports*, I-IX, New Haven 1929-1946.

——, *Caravan cities*, Oxford 1932.

Rostovtzeff, M. I. and others (eds.), "Dura and the problem of Parthian art", *Yale Classical Studies* 5, 1935, 157-304.
——, *Dura-Europos and its art*, Oxford 1938.
Rowland, B., *Art and architecture of India*, London 1952.
Safar, F. and Mustafa, M. A., *Hatra: the city of the Sun God* (in Arabic), Baghdad 1974.
Savage, E., *Seleucia-on-the-Tigris*, Ann Arbor 1977.
Schippmann, K., *Die iranischen Feuerheiligtümer*, Berlin 1971.
Schlumberger, D., *La Palmyrène du nord-ouest*, Paris 1951.
——, "Descendants non méditerranéens de l'art grec", *Syria* 37, 1960, 131-166, 253-319.
——, "The excavations at Surkh Kotal", *Proceedings of the British Academy* 47, 1961, 77-95.
——, *L'orient hellénisé*, Paris 1970.
——, "Les quatre tribus de Palmyre", *Syria* 48, 1971, 121-133.
Schneider, C., *Kulturgeschichte des Hellenismus*, I, Munich 1967.
Segal, J. B., "New mosaics from Edessa", *Archaeology* 12 (3), autumn 1959, 150-157.
——, *Edessa, the Blessed City*, Oxford 1970.
Seyrig, H., "Antiquités syriennes", articles in *Syria* 13, 1932 - 48, 1971.
——, *Antiquités syriennes*, I-VI, Paris 1934-1966.
——, "Le repas des morts et le 'Banquet funèbre' à Palmyre", *AAS* 1, 1951, 32-40.
——, "Plaquettes votives de terre cuite", *AAS* 1, 1951, 147-156.
Seyrig, H., Amy, R. and Will, E., *Le sanctuaire de Bel à Palmyre* (forthcoming).
Spuler, B. and others (eds.), "Der Hellenistische Orient", *Handbuch der Orientalistik* 7, IV (forthcoming).
Starcky, J., *Inventaire des inscriptions de Palmyre*, X, Damascus 1949.
——, "Autour d'une dédicace palmyrénienne à Šadrafa et à Duʿanat", *Syria* 26, 1949, 43-85.
Starcky, J. and Munajjed, S., *Palmyre*, Paris 1952.
Stark, K. S., *Personal names in Palmyrene inscriptions*, Oxford 1971.
Stein, M. A., *Old routes of western Īrân*, London 1940.
Tarn, W. W., *The Greeks in Bactria and India*, 2nd edn., Cambridge 1951.
Tarn, W. W. and Griffith, G. T., *Hellenistic civilization*, 3rd edn., London 1952.
Teixidor, J., *Inventaire des inscriptions de Palmyre*, XI, Beirut 1965.
——, "Bulletin d'épigraphie sémitique", *Syria* 44, 1967 - 49, 1972.
——, *The pagan god. Popular religion in the Greco-Roman near east*, Leiden 1977.
Will, E., *Histoire politique de monde hellénistique*, I, II, Nancy 1966, 1967.
Wright, G. R. H., "The significance of the square temple in Iran", in: Kiani, M. Y. (ed.), *VIth International Congress of Iranian art and archaeology*, Teheran 1976, 335-348.
Wroth, W. W., *A catalogue of the Greek coins in the British Museum, 23: Parthia*, London 1903.
Young, J. H., "Commagenian tiaras, royal and divine", *AJA* 68, 1964, 29-34.
Zaehner, R. C., *The dawn and twilight of Zoroastrianism*, London 1961.

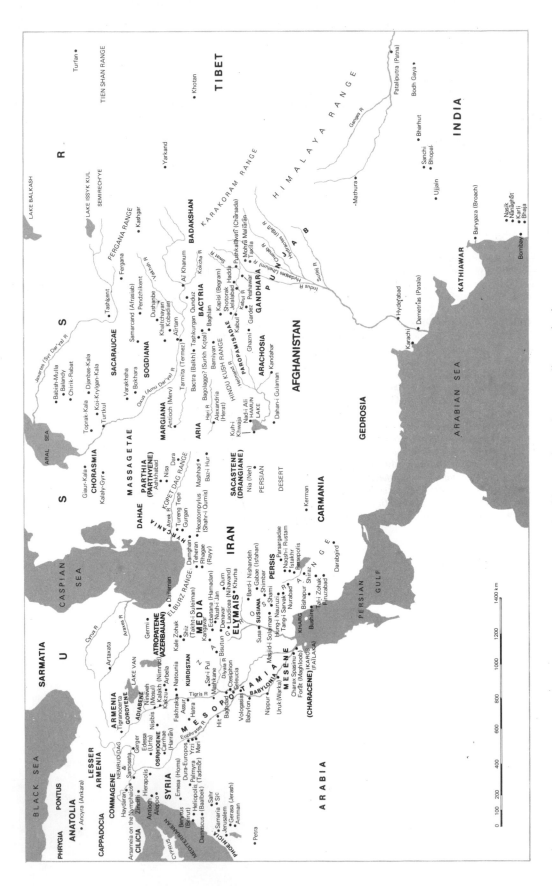

Map of the Parthian empire and surrounding territories

INTRODUCTION

1. The history of the Parthians

The Parthians were an Iranian people who dominated near eastern history during the half millennium that extended from the mid-third century B.C. to the 220s A.D. From their beginnings east of the Caspian Sea they created an empire whose heartland lay in the mountains, plains and deserts of Iran, to which they added the rich alluvial terrain of Mesopotamia, including Babylonia; but the repercussions of their coming were felt in territories beyond, in desert and cultivated Syria, in the Anatolian hills, in south Russia and eastwards across Afghanistan and the range of the Hindu Kush (see Map). Thus their conquests and their impact extended over an area that had already had a long and complex previous history. Mesopotamia and Syria, lands of the Semites, had seen the rise of local empires, of which the greatest had been that of the Assyrians; by the first millennium B.C. Aramaeans, and latterly Arabs, were increasingly influential here. Astral deities loomed large in the Semitic religions, represented in anthropomorphic guise or indicated by beasts or symbols; other objects held sacred by some were trees, and special stones (baetyls). In the meantime, however, Iranians had been filtering southwards from a nomadic existence on the Russian steppes into Iran, where they settled. By the sixth century B.C. one group, the Persians, had become powerful enough under their kings of Achaemenid line first to crush their rivals, the Medes, and then to embark on a career of conquest that eventually brought them a domain that stretched from Egypt and Anatolia across Semitic Syria and Mesopotamia and over the Iranian territories to the Punjab. The main cultural impact of these Achaemenian Persians was concentrated in their own homeland, the southwest of Iran, where they developed a culture of mixed Iranian, Semitic and Greek elements and erected their greatest palace complex at Persepolis; coinage was introduced. Ahura Mazda was their greatest god, worshipped apparently in the open.

Great as the Persian empire was, it was nevertheless conquered in its turn by the youthful Greek king Alexander the Great, leading his Macedonian and Greek soldiery; Persepolis was burnt. After Alexander's untimely death in 323 B.C. his general Seleucus seized the Asiatic territories lying between the east Mediterranean and Afghanistan, and proclaimed himself king of this Seleucid empire. He promoted Alexander's policies of settling Greeks and introducing Hellenic culture along routes of communication, and of generally merging Hellenic and oriental. Coinage was reformed, along established Greek lines. With the Greeks came their deities, again customarily shown anthropomorphically or represented by animals or symbols in the Greeks' remarkably naturalistic art styles, as statuary in the round, in relief or in painting or mosaic. Religious ceremonies included sacrifices at open-air altars, behind which a temple, usually a rectangular hall with a pillared entrance and often a surrounding colonnade, might be erected to house statuary and offerings.

The Seleucids' resources were overstretched, and from the mid-third century B.C. onwards their grip on these far-flung territories progressively weakened. Significant seizures of independence by local rulers occurred in three main areas. The first was Asia Minor, where eventually such eastern Iranized regions as Armenia, Cappadocia and later Commagene broke away; these ultimately fell victim to Roman eastward territorial expansion. The second was Afghanistan, where the ancient satrapy (province) of Bactria became an independent Greco-Bactrian kingdom under Diodotus I c. 239-238 B.C. (Pl.XVIIh). For two remarkable centuries dynasties of Greek origin maintained themselves in this distant region; their coin issues constitute the main evidence for their fluctuating fortunes. North of the Hindu Kush Greco-Bactrian rulers such as Euthydemus II even for a time seized parts of south Russia, but eventually by c. 135 B.C. the possessions of the last king, Heliocles, were being overrun by encroaching nomad tribes which included a strong Iranian element moving south from central Asia. Meanwhile, however, south of the Hindu Kush other Hellenic dynasts, the Indo-Greeks or rather Indo-Bactrians, had taken over yet further regions of southern Afghanistan and north-west India, most notably Gandhara and its great city of Taxila. Here such monarchs as the great Menander and the long-lived Strato held sway, until ousted in their turn by Indo-Scythians of central Asian Iranian nomad origin, temporarily by Maues and permanently, perhaps in 57 B.C., by Azes I. Around the turn of our era these were supplanted by Indo-Parthian rulers, of whom the most famous was Gondophares (c. A.D. 20-46?). From the mid-first century A.D., however, the whole region from central Asia to northern India was welded for two centuries into an empire by the Kushans, again of Iranian kinship, whose most towering dynast was Kanishka I (c. A.D. 120s-c. 151?). Thus the area was one of an extraordinary cultural mix, with the dominant group at any one period providing the main emphasis. The Greek religious element, visible most clearly on Greco-Bactrian coins, lasted well into subsequent eras (Pl. XVII); the Iranian inheritance was strong, and the two great Indian religions, polytheistic Hinduism and the more intellectual Buddhism, naturally made their presence felt, especially south of the Hindu Kush.

The third breakaway, and the one most deadly for the Seleucids, was that of the Parthians. Their half-millennium of history has to be studied from poor, and often foreign, documentation. Evidence from areas under Parthian control include the buildings and artefacts of inhabited sites, inscriptions, parchments, papyri and coins. Surviving lengthy literary accounts were written mostly in the Mediterranean area under Roman control, by men such as Polybius, Strabo, Isidorus of Charax, Josephus, Plutarch, Tacitus, Arrian, Philostratus and Cassius Dio, who all too often reflect Roman governmental hostility. Further information may be found in Jewish, Syriac and Chinese writings, but later Armenian, Persian, Indian and Arab accounts embody considerable fantasy.

Trouble seemingly began here with independent action by Andragoras, Seleucid governor of the east Caspian province of Parthia (or 'Parthyene'), about 250 B.C., when the Seleucid king was occupied elsewhere. A semi-nomadic Iranian tribe named the Parni or Aparni was in the area, and under their leader Arshak (called Arsaces by westerners) soon ousted Andragoras and occupied the province of Parthia, whose name they adopted for themselves and later for their empire. This seizure occurred perhaps in 247 B.C., the year from which the Parthians later reckoned their own era, or 239/8 B.C. They created a capital at Nisa. Arsaces' successor allegedly pushed southwards into Iran, but Parthian advance was halted by the Seleucids until the earlier second century B.C., when Seleucid disarray allowed the defection of the Iranian provinces of Media, Persis and Elymais and then a renewed Parthian onslaught under Mithradates I (*c.* 171-138 B.C.) which carried the Parthians westwards to Babylonia. By now the Parthians were issuing coins, which owed much to Seleucid models and moneyers (Pl. XVIh-jj). About 138-124 B.C., however, east Iran was overrun and settled by Saka nomads from central Asia; it was renamed Sacastene, and in the first century B.C. its Indo-Scythian rulers were instrumental in ending Indo-Bactrian rule in Gandhara. Meanwhile Parthian fortunes recovered under the dynamic Mithradates II (*c.* 124/3-87 B.C.), who added northern Mesopotamia, including Dura-Europos (*c.* 113 B.C.?), to the realm (Pl. XVIk); most significantly, in 96-95 B.C. his ambassador met Sulla, general of the expanding western state of Republican Rome, and the Euphrates became the frontier between the Roman and Parthian empires. In 64 B.C. the Romans annexed what was left of the Seleucid domains as their province of Syria. So the Parthian and Roman empires henceforward became neighbours. Their co-existence was punctuated at intervals by hostilities, a situation which continued after the Republican system of government at Rome had been replaced by the one-man rule of the emperors, beginning with Augustus (30 B.C. - A.D. 14); one continuing bone of contention was Armenia, which each side wished to dominate. From the turn of our era onwards disputes over succession to the Parthian throne became frequent enough to damage governmental interests. The coinage deteriorated in quality (Pl. XVIn-yy). Regions such as the kingdoms of Hatra and Characene (Pl. XVIIc,d) in north and south Mesopotamia respectively acquired local autonomy, and from A.D. 164-6 portions of northern Mesopotamia, including Dura-Europos, were acquired permanently by the Romans. Finally, in the 220s A.D., Ardashir, vassal ruler of Persis (cf. Pl. XVIIyy), overthrew the feeble Parthian kings Artabanus V, Artavasdes (Pl. XVIyy) and the last Vologases and seized their empire, of which his dynasty, the Sasanid, now became the masters; his successor conquered the Kushans.

Thus the Parthian empire contained elements from Iranian, Semitic and Greek cultures, all intermingled, and varying in proportion from place to place and period to period. Sources of wealth were agriculture and a through caravan trade. The monarchy was absolute in theory, but in practice royal power depended on numerous factors such as access to funds, the co-operation of the baronial feudal Iranian lords and vassal kings and the acquiescence of the cities (cf. Pl. XVIIgg). The king's subjects in Iran were mostly Iranians, but in Mesopotamia they were primarily Semites of various kinds including Aramaeans, Jews and Arabs, and throughout the empire there was a considerable population whose ultimately Greek origin long remained influential. Thus although the Parthians' own Iranian language, written heterographically in Aramaic but with Iranian endings, entered official use, Greek remained an important administrative language (Pl. XVIjj-yy); although the Parthians had their own era, the Seleucid era continued in official use throughout for dating documents (Pl. XVIjj). Similar mixtures of old and new characterized the whole of Parthian government, society, architecture and art. In these ways the Parthians maintained themselves as a power for half a millennium at the centre of a sphere of Iranian influence that reached Asia Minor in the west and, to the east, northern India.

2. *The religions of the Parthian empire*

The theologies and cult practices that existed in the Parthian empire are difficult to discern because of scanty contemporary documentation. Some lengthy oriental texts of apparent relevance do survive, but these date from the succeeding Sasanian era and their contents are therefore highly suspect. Furthermore, during the five hundred years of Parthian history religious changes must have taken place, but these are not clearly marked in the little surviving evidence. Perhaps it would be easiest to attempt here to establish in broad outline firstly the main religious preoccupations of the three principal population groups, Iranian, Semitic and Greek, secondly the amount of intermingling between these, and thirdly the extent to which outside religions had a rôle to play.

The Iranian population seems to have had a considerable religious inheritance from the later Achemenian era. This included a reverence for several deities, the supreme god Ahura Mazda (favoured by the rulers), Mithra, originally the god of contracts, and Anahita, goddess of fecundity, as well as for the king's 'soul' or *fravashi* (in Greek, *daimon*). The priesthood of the Magi was prominent in ritual, in which a bundle of rods (*barsom*) and perhaps the intoxicating liquid *haoma* were used. Achaemenian religion, at first outside (later perhaps inside) royal and Magian circles, was seemingly affected by an Iranian prophet, Zarathushtra (Zoroaster), whose teaching included belief in the conflict between Ahura Mazda, regarded as a god of good, and his evil adversary Ahriman. Ordinary villagers favoured fertility cults. Fire, streams and mountains were also revered, and horse sacrifice occurred. Burial practices included both inhumation (in royal circles) and exposure of human corpses. In the Parthian era all these beliefs and practices seem to have continued, although doubtless as previously with varying emphases being placed upon each component according to region and to section of the population, whether royalty, vassal monarchs, feudal lords, priests, townsfolk, villagers or nomads. Ahura Mazda (Ohrmazd) is still venerated, as Oromasdes, in the important religious inscriptions of Commagene from the mid-first century B.C., and, as Ooromozdo, on Kushan coins of two centuries later. Mithra seemingly enjoyed widespread popularity; he too appears in the Commagene texts and on Kushan coins; his name commonly forms a theophoric element in names of kings and commoners in the Parthian period, and both the Commagenian inscriptions and the Greco-Roman geographer Strabo (XV, 3, 13 = 732) of the late first century B.C. give the valuable information that Mithra was by then identified with the sun. As for Anahita, western authors such as Polybius (X, 27), Isidorus of Charax (6) and Aelian (*De Natura Animalium*, XII, 23) mention her temples at Ecbatana and in Elymais in west Iran, and others her popularity in Asia Minor. The king's spirit was still honoured, as a Greek inscription of Susa honouring the *daimon* of one of the kings named Phraates and other Greek texts of Commagene make clear. The importance of the priestly Magi and the continuing use of the sacred bundle of rods (*barsom*) are evident from Strabo (XV, 3,15 = 733) and Pausanias (V, 27, 5), while the latter mentions *haoma* (as *omomi*). Zoroastrianism must have been evolving, but its rôle is obscure; the Sasanian Dênkart (Madan, 412) says a king Vologases collected surviving texts, but the Sasanians did not regard the Parthians as orthodox. Yet a generally Zoroastrian climate is perhaps indicated by the use of Zoroastrian months in documents from Nisa and Avroman, by the element Arta, 'Rectitude', in royal names, and by such personal names at Nisa as Ohrmazdik and

Dinmazdak. The cult of fire was clearly of great significance: Isidorus of Charax (11) says that not far from Nisa, in the town of Asaak 'where Arsaces was first proclaimed king', there burned an everlasting fire, both Strabo (XV, 3,15 = 733) and Pausanias describe the fire ceremonies of Anatolia, and Fire appears as a god (Athsho) on Kushan coins. As regards streams, the river Oxus is named as a god (Okhsho) on coins of the Kushan king Kanishka, and mountains are revealed as possessing deities by the Roman historian Tacitus (XII, 13). An eschatological belief in the ascent of the soul to paradise is set out in the post-Parthian Zoroastrian literature or Avesta, and this may have grown up earlier; discoveries of tombs and sarcophagi from Nisa across Iran to Mesopotamia and Syria testify to the widespread popularity of inhumation as a form of burial, while the testimony of Strabo and Justin together with finds of ossuaries east of the Caspian Sea at Nisa and in Sogdiane demonstrate the continuation of the exposure of corpses. But despite the strength of Iranian religious tradition, some innovations are discernible within it. Firstly Verethraghna, god of victory, joins the pantheon; he is called Artagnes in the Commagene texts and Oshlagno on Kushan coinage, and appears in theophoric names at Nisa and Dura-Europos. Secondly rulers, inspired by Hellenistic Greek practice, promoted the worship of their own dynastic ancestors at great shrines; the texts accompanying the great *hierothesia* of Commagenian royalty of the mid-first century B.C. provide the clearest testimony, while other shrines, such as that at Iranian Shami or those in the Kushan realm, may have played the same rôle.

Very different were the religions of the indigenous populations of Parthian Mesopotamia, and of adjoining areas of Syria. Here lived Semitic peoples, complex in their culture and their religious affiliations. Many primitive kinds of cult survived, such as those of high places, of water in its manifestations as springs, rivers, lakes, wells and the sea, of trees and of sacred stones called *beth-el* ('house of god', in Greek *baetyla*). On a higher plane there were deities conceived of more in human terms, often accompanied or symbolized by creatures from the animal kingdom. These included the innumerable local divinities of the Semitic world, the *baal* and *baalat* ('Lord' and 'Lady') of a particular area, or the individual deity, often called the Gad or *gny* (guardian spirit), of a town or village.

Astral elements loomed large, furthermore; deities of the sky, of the sun and moon, of the morning and evening star, and a great goddess were commonplace, whose tasks were often to produce fertility through rain and good harvests, and their character frequently remained much the same although their names might vary from place to place. The concept of the sacred area, or *haram*, belonging to a divinity or tomb, was also strong (cf. Pl. I). Semites also believed strongly in an afterlife and customarily made provision for the dead, through inhumation and the donation of food, trinkets and other items. Such were the generalities. At any one Semitic centre a number of cults was present, and these often included ones that had originated in other Semitic cultures. Thus in Seleucid and certainly for long in Parthian Babylonia documents, theophoric names, the continuance of sanctuaries and occasional literary references indicate that the old Babylonian divinities Marduk, Nebu, Anu, Nanai and Ishtar were still reverenced. In northern Mesopotamia and desert Syria evidence from the mid- to later Parthian periods, primarily epigraphical, paints a picture of great cultural complexity. The inscriptions of Hatra, for instance, reveal the worship of Babylonian Nebu, Nergal and Nanai, west Semitic Baᶜalshamîn (the Lord of Heaven) and Atarᶜatê (Atargatis; Hadad also may be represented sculpturally) together with Arab deities, who are in the majority: Shahiru, the goddess Allât, and what are apparently two separate deities both addressed as Our Lord (Marên), one of whom is associated with an eagle and is probably a god of heaven, and the other of whom is Shamash the sun god, who forms a triad together with Our Lady (Martên—a moon goddess?) and the Dionysus-like Son of Our Lord (Bar-Marên). Just such mixtures of deities from differing Semitic origins, Arab, Mesopotamian and west Semitic, are found at other sites of the area, notably Edessa, Dura-Europos and Palmyra. The Edessenes worshipped Babylonian Nebû and also the supreme god Bel, as well as such Arab deities as Shamash, ʿAzîzû, Munʿîm and Nahî. At Dura-Europos under Parthian and then Roman control there were devotees of the town's own spirit or Gad, the deities Aphlad and Azzanathkona apparently from the nearby Euphrates village of Anath, the Gad and Iarhibôl from Palmyra, west Semitic Baʿalshamin, Hadad, Atargatis and Adonis, Babylonian Bel, Nanai and Nebû, Arab Arsû, Asherû and Saʿad, and probably others as well who are not specifically mentioned in surviving texts but may be portrayed in art. Even richer was the religious life of Palmyra, in Roman Syria and therefore outside Parthian control but linked culturally to these west-Parthian Semitic regions: objects of worship comprised the spring Efqa, sacred stones and trees, and divinities including the Palmyrene solar Iarhibôl, lunar ʿAglibôl, Malakbel with his vegetation and solar aspects and local spirits called Gad and *ginnayê*, together with Babylonian Bel, Beltî, Nebû, Nergal and goddesses Ishtar and Nanai, west Semitic Baʿalshamîn, Belhammôn, Shadrafâ, Elqônerâ and Atargatis, Arab Shamash, Maʿan(û), Shaʿar(û), Abgal, Rahm, Arsû, ʿAzîzû and goddesses Allat and Manôt, and, most exceptionally for these Semitic regions, Iranian Anahita, although she was of little significance at Palmyra; a curiosity of Palmyrene theology was the frequent grouping, from roughly the turn of our era onwards, of deities into pairs such as Arsû and ʿAzîzû, triads like that apparently of Bel, Iarhibôl and ʿAglibôl or the possible one of Baʿalshamîn, ʿAglibôl and Malakbel, or larger groupings such as that of the *ginnayê*. The inscriptions and monuments of Palmyra also provide unusual insights into eschatological beliefs: corpses were often mummified, the afterlife is sometimes connected with sun worship, funerary banquets were held, and the soul or *nefesh* of the dead was thought to inhabit a monument, a stone or effigy, allotted to it.

The religions of this vast Semitic area developed in several respects in the Hellenistic and Parthian eras. Firstly, the old Akkadian title Bel ('Lord') of Babylonian Marduk now became used as the name of a high god, of widespread popularity. Secondly, the grouping of deities, particularly into the pairs and triads visible notably at Hatra and Palmyra, from the turn of our era onwards, may have constituted local interpretations of developments in Babylonian astral theology during the Hellenistic period; the formation of a great triad at Roman-period Baalbek was doubtless related to this process. Thirdly, as part of these Babylonian astral speculations, the pseudo-science of astrology was evolved. Fourthly the frequent occurrence of benches in Semitic shrines doubtless indicates that ritual dining took place here. Lastly it is noteworthy that the influence of Iranian religion in this Semitic area was minimal.

The invading Greeks brought with them their own deities and religious beliefs and practices, profoundly different again from those of the east. By Alexander's time a welter of older and newer nature, regional, tribal, sky and social divinities together with spirits and personified abstractions such as Justice had been roughly organized into a fairly hierarchical system; despite their all too human characteristics and failings, recorded in myths and legends, these deities were regarded as responsible for human affairs and morality. As mount Olympus was reputedly their home, they were known as Olympians. Heading the system was Zeus, father of gods and men, protector of law and morals, whose consort was his sister Hera, like him the child of the ousted Kronos. The divine state Zeus ruled mirrored that of late Bronze Age ('Mycenaean') Greek society, with a monarch constantly challenged by recalcitrant underlings, who were responsible for different areas of human activity. Other leading Olympians were also regarded mythologically as children of Kronos: Poseidon, god of water and particularly the sea, Hades, the grim lord of the underworld, Demeter the corn-goddess and Hestia, goddess of the hearth. Zeus himself was said to have produced five important divine offspring: the virgin Athena, protectress of cities and goddess of war and arts, the likewise virgin Artemis, huntress and goddess of birth and prosperity, her allegedly twin brother Apollo, responsible for the civilized arts and morality, the martial Ares, and the orgiastic Dionysus, later particularly the god of wine. Further members of the Olympian pantheon included the sun god Helios, Hermes who acted as divine messenger, god of fertility and guide of souls to the underworld, Zeus' daughter Aphrodite, the goddess of love and fertility, and her young associate Eros, god of sexual passion. To these were added deities which personified abstract ideas, such as Nike (Victory) or places; these were usually goddesses. The originally superhuman hero Heracles, famous for his strength and courage and for his exploits including the Twelve Labours, was also increasingly worshipped as a god. Secret cults, or mysteries, also existed, embodying mystic ideas: thus the originally agrarian Eleusinian mysteries, in which Demeter figured prominently, offered initiates various rewards, the Orphic, in which Dionysus was important, offered a happy after-life to purified initiates, and Dionysus' own cult acquired some mystic characteristics. Cults of superhuman heroes also became common. Ceremonies centred around sacrifice, the making of a gift to the gods; this could be vegetable or animal, made to divinities, heroes or the dead in public or private, and consist of a communal meal, libation, or burnt or buried offering, often made at or on an open-air altar, and often accompanied by music. The dead were buried or cremated and their souls were believed to live on in the underworld, Hades; that this belief was carried east by the Greeks is suggested by the occurrence at the originally Greek city of Seleucia on the Tigris of the specifically Greek practice of placing a coin in the mouth of the deceased, which in Greek terms represented payment to the underworld ferryman, Charon. During the Hellenistic period there were several developments relevant to the east. Some cults assumed greater importance, such as those of Dionysus, of Aphrodite, of Helios, identified with Apollo, and of Heracles, sometimes called Kallinikos, the 'victorious'; that of Tyche, good or bad 'Fortune', sometimes became attached to a particular city so as to personify its luck. Twelve leading Olympians from among those just mentioned were sometimes incorporated into a special group of Twelve Gods, the Dodecatheoi, although the precise list of names tended to vary slightly. Among the cults of superhuman heroes those of city founders were important. Alexander the Great demanded, and got, his own divinity recognized by the Greek cities, and so introduced from the east something that was new in the Greek world, the politically motivated ruler-cult; the Seleucids, perhaps from Antiochus I (281-261 B.C.) onwards, followed suit by establishing a cult of the reigning king and his ancestors.

Given the successive dominations of the Iranian and Mesopotamian areas by Greeks and Parthians, the intermingling that took place between the religions of masters and subjects was perhaps less than might been expected. The oriental religions, Iranian and Semitic, seem to have preserved their own character and boundaries to a remarkable degree. Certainly, Iranian Anahita was mentioned on two religious tokens or *tesserae* at Semitic Roman Palmyra, and Babylonian Nanai evidently had a certain popularity in Iranian regions, for she possessed temples at Susa and also at the Parthian capital Nisa as documents there of the first century B.C. indicate, and later she was mentioned on coins of the Kushan king Kanishka. But such oriental interchanges seem to have been infrequent. Quite the reverse was true, however, of the kinds of intermingling that occurred between the Greek and oriental cults. These were clearly of a different and profounder kind, as numerous documents show. The first involved the finding of equivalences between leading Greek and oriental deities, or syncretism. Correspondences between Iranian and Greek divinities are stated explicitly in the Commagenian Greek texts of the mid-first century B.C., where Ahura Mazda has become the composite god Zeus-Oromasdes, Mithra one component of Apollo-Mithras-Helios-Hermes, and Verethraghna one of Artagnes-Heracles-Ares; earlier Hellenistic Greek inscriptions from Persepolis addressed to Zeus the Greatest (Megistos), Apollo Helios and Artemis Athena, make little sense in a Greek religious context but would fit well into an Iranian one if Ahura Mazda and Mithra (as named in Commagene) and perhaps Anahita are meant. Equivalences between the Greek and the more numerous Semitic deities indicated by bilingual and other texts and representations were slightly less fixed and embodied some overlapping. Thus among male deities Bel and Baʿalshamîn were both addressed as Zeus, although Baʿalshamîn in particular is often distinguished by epithets such as Kyrios, 'the Lord'; Nebû becomes Apollo, and Nergal Heracles. As for goddesses, Nanai and Azzanathcona were equated with Artemis, as was Allat in a text of 6 B.C. at Palmyra, but Allat was normally translated as Athena; Gad could be represented and addressed at Dura-Europos as Tyche, seated like the famous Tyche statue of Antioch, but with the lions of Atargatis or Astarte at her side, while Atarʿatê herself simply has her name westernized as Atargatis. The ancient Syrian religious was called Semeion by Lucian (*De Syria Dea*, 33). The second kind of intermingling between Greek and oriental was that where a Greek deity was adopted by a local population and worshipped under its Greek name in the eastern language, as was Nemesis at Palmyra and probably at Dura-Europos also. Thirdly the rise to prominence within Iranian religion of Verethraghna and the worship of deceased royal ancestors was surely due to the impact of the Greek Heracles and ruler-cults.

To east and west, the fringes of the Iranian world were in contact with alien religions. The successive rulers of Bactria and the Punjab, both Greek and Iranian, had to take account of the existence within their borders of two great Indian religions, each of whose adherents sought through right conduct to be absorbed after death into the changeless state of *nirvana*. The more ancient of these was polytheistic Hinduism, with its worship of spirits, powers of nature, ancient gods such as Indra the chief deity, the sky god Varuna, the solar Mitra and the fire god Agni, and the trinity, formed around the turn of our era, of Brahma, creator of the universe, the kind Vishnu and the terrible Śiva, god of destruction; around 500 B.C. the Buddha introduced a more humanistic and spiritual way to this end, Buddhism, which continued to develop and gain in popularity through the succeeding centuries. Recognition of these Indian religions by Greek and Kushan rulers may be seen in coin designs and legends; both the Greek king Menander and the Kushan Kanishka were remembered favourably in Buddhist tradition. To the west, Dura-Europos under Roman rule (*c.* A.D. 165-256) yielded testimony of the presence of several important religions of the Roman empire: the cults of the Roman standards, of north Syrian Jupiter Dolichenus, and of the originally Iranian Mithra westernized as the very different saviour god Mithras with his myth centring on the slaughter of primeval bull, together with Christianity, and a kind of Judaism that permitted synagogue walls to be painted with Biblical scenes in apparent defiance of the Jewish Second commandment against the making of images. Hebrew and Roman documentation indicates a large Jewish community in Parthian Mesopotamia generally; and an inscription of Palmyra mentions a temple of the deified Roman Augusti in the Babylonian trading town of Vologasias.

3. *Religious and funerary architecture of the Parthian empire*

By the time the Greeks took over Iran and Mesopotamia, western Asiatic architectural traditions had been developing for millennia. Transport difficulties ensured that it was normal to use materials from the locality. Earth could form floors or walls, or be used to make the popular medium of mud-brick; clay was employed as flooring, mortar or decoration, or was used for fired brick; wood, where available, provided lintels, doors, column shafts and roof beams; of western Asiatic stones, laborious to move and carve, limestone was that in commonest use, for paving, flooring, some walling, and occasionally for roofing and ornament.

Most of the components and techniques of building had already had a long history. Individual rooms, building complexes and indeed some urban areas all normally had rectangular layouts. Certain brick-laying techniques had lasted for millennia. Some sizable halls, particularly in Iran, might be filled with pillars or columns to support the roof. The roofing itself would normally be of wooden beams laid flat from wall to wall and covered with earth or clay, or else of simple brick vaults with the bricks laid either radially so as to follow the long axis of the room, or across the long axis of the chamber in the pitched brick method. Exterior mud brick walling was often given decorative patterns.

Greek architecture, and temples in particular, exemplified a different approach. Although mud-brick, clay and wood were in use, buildings of the greatest significance would, wherever feasible, be of stone, normally limestone or the plentiful Greek white marble, carved into rectangular blocks held in position by metal clamps. The most essential cult item was the open-air altar, normally rectangular. Where a temple was built it stood behind the altar, and its purpose was to house religious statuary and treasures. The temple usually consisted of a rectangular hall standing on a three-step base entered from the centre of one short side, often with a surrounding colonnade, or peristyle. The roofs were ridged, normally supported by wooden beams and covered by terracotta tiles; the triangular gable ends, or pediments, often contained figured decoration. Architectural proportions and ornament were worked out according to one of three systems or orders, the plain Doric, the Ionic with its volute column capitals, and the Corinthian, like the Ionic but with capitals bearing acanthus and volute decoration. The Greeks carried these ideas into Asia, where they also promoted the use of lime and gypsum mortar, and plaster.

Under Seleucid and Parthian rule religious structures continued to embody Semitic, Iranian and Hellenic traditions; there was some intermingling, and some innovations appeared. The oldest type of sanctuary still in use was the so-called 'broad-room' temple, popular throughout Mesopotamia since the third millennium B.C. and consisting of a transverse chamber with a niche set centrally in the back wall, often entered through a vestibule and set in a court, which might have other chambers around. In forms ranging from pure to adulterated it recurred all over Seleucid and Parthian Mesopotamia, in Seleucid Iran with the 'temple of Heracles' at Masjid-i Solaiman, and even in early Seleucid Bactria at Aï Khanum (Pls. II, cf. Va). Old stepped towers, or ziggurats, were refurbished at Uruk, Nippur and Assur; and the towers, buttresses, and gateway and roof terraces reached by staircases that characterized many Mesopotamian and Syrian temples (notably at Dura-Europos) seem also to have been derived from Babylonian temple forms. A less ancient form of cult building, created perhaps early in the first millennium B.C., was the squarish tower with internal stairs or ramp, often thought to have been associated with fire ceremonies; the tower-like structures at early Parthian Nisa, to the rear of the Jandial temple at Indo-Scythian Taxila (Pl. IIIa, D) and attached behind the central temple complex of late Parthian Hatra (Pl. IIIb) could be continuations of this form. A special kind of squarish tower, again with ramps or staircases inside, but with a rectangular projection on each face, was in use in Media by the eighth century B.C., and this recurred at early Parthian Hecatompylus (Shahr-i Qumis). Three types of structure, perhaps, were contributed by Achaemenian Iran. The first was the large open-air terrace on the side or top of a hill; examples in use during the Seleucid and Parthian periods include the sanctuaries of Masjid-i Solaiman and Bard-i Nishandeh in south-west Iran, the Commagenian dynastic shrine of Nemrud Dağ (Pl. VIc) and the possibly dynastic complexes at Shami in Iran and Surkh Kotal in Afghanistan. The second, the walled open-air enclosure, could be combined with the terrace. The third was the 'centralized square' hall with four internal columns arranged in a square, surrounded by corridors. The Gate of Xerxes at Persepolis provides one Achaemenian antecedent for this; a clearer parallel in a building at Susa usually considered Achaemenian may, however, perhaps date from the Seleucid era (Pl. IIIa, A). Whatever its precise origins it spread widely throughout western Asia particularly as a temple form, and remained in use throughout the Seleucid and Parthian periods (Pls. III, IVb). The religious structures brought with them by the invading Greeks had a lesser impact. Their main temple type, the rectangular 'long room' hall entered from one short end, with gabled roof and usually surrounded by a colonnade and raised on a three-step platform, was used c. 250 B.C. for a Doric and an Ionic shrine on the Persian Gulf island of Ikaros (Failaka) and a Seleucid chapel of Artemis at Dura-Europos and it plainly influenced the Indo-Scythian Jandial temple at Taxila and the Kushan square temple at Surkh Kotal, Afghanistan (cf. Pl. Va). In its Hellenistic and east Roman forms, moreover, this essentially Hellenic type affected the design of Palmyrene temples (Pl. Va) and at least two limestone temples of Parthian Hatra (Pl. IIIb, C, D). A rarer Greek form, the circular drum-like hall with conical roof and surrounding columns known as a *tholos*, may have inspired the circularity of the Round Hall at early Parthian Nisa. The adding of little theatres to religious complexes at Parthian Seleucia and also at Dura-Europos had Mediterranean parallels from the Hellenistic period onwards. Greeks also improved a cave for the worship of Heracles at Karafto, west Iran. The Parthian period itself saw an important innovation in both religious and secular architecture in the creation of the open-fronted vaulted hall or *iwan* of brick or stone; of obscure origin, it was used in Mesopotamia from the earlier first century A.D., sometimes in juxtaposed groups of two or three (Pls. IIIb, IVc), sometimes with one or two facing their pairs across a court, and from the third century A.D. onwards achieved enormous popularity in Sasanian and Islamic building. The alien religions practised on the fringes of the Parthian world also had their special architectural forms. To the east the monuments of Buddhism were prominent, with as a characteristic type the circular relic mound or *stupa*, frequently raised on a square base and covered lavishly with reliefs. To the west, Roman-period Dura-Europos witnessed the conversion of houses for the purposes of imported cults: one was turned into a benched Mithraic shrine, another into a Christian baptistry and a third into a Jewish synagogue (Pl. XLVIII).

A certain amount of intermingling took place between the elements of Iranian, Semitic and Hellenic religious architecture under Seleucid and Parthian rule. This was of different kinds. A temple type might be carried far from home: of course the shrines raised in the Greek manner were all instances of this, but there were further examples such as the erection of temples of Babylonian style by the Greeks of Aï Khanum in Afghanistan. Or again, elements from different traditions might be blended, as happened with the Indo-Scythian temple of Jandial, Taxila, where its overall proportions and Ionic order were Hellenic but within this were incorporated perhaps a square tower and certainly an Iranian 'centralized square' cella and corridors (Pl. IIIa, D). Architectural ornament from different traditions, too, might be blended on the same monument. In Parthian Mesopotamia a practice grew up of adding geometric designs in white stucco to the outsides and insides of buildings, normally those of brick: often picked out in colours, this work was capable of creating rich effects.

How far were particular building types reserved exclusively for certain religions or deities? The only sure evidence for identification consists of inscriptions, together with such literary testimony as exists; other kinds of evidence, notably artistic, are often difficult to interpret. The richest epigraphic information is that from earlier Parthian Nisa, and later from Dura-Europos and Hatra, as well as from Palmyra in Roman Syria, and the Kushan realm of Afghanistan and north India. This, when put together with other evidence, indicates that the alien religions of Buddhism, Roman Mithraism, Christianity and Judaism, which all made special architectural demands, had these demands fulfilled as far as was practical. But how far was this true of the Iranian, Semitic and Hellenic polytheism of western Asia? It has been suggested on the tenuous basis of the material from the religious terraces of Masjid-i Solaiman and Bard-i Nishandeh that Ahura Mazda was worshipped here, and elsewhere, on an open-air podium; but this is as yet unconfirmed. Those Iranian cults, perhaps including this, which involved the worship of fire would have needed the regular provision of special chambers to house it, such as the *pyraitheia* mentioned by Strabo (XV, 3,15 = 733) or the later *ateshgah*, and possibly sometimes to exhibit it also. But in the main it would seem, rather, that as regards Iranian, Semitic and Greek cults there was no necessity for there to be any close connection between deity and sanctuary type. On the one hand divinities of widely different origins were happy to dwell in sanctuaries of broadly the same kinds. Thus a variety of Semitic and Greek deities at Dura-Europos or Hatra, for instance, as well as probably Greek or

Iranian deities at Masjid-i Solaiman, occupied similar temples of essentially Babylonian 'broad room' type. Conversely, one particular cult might be housed in structures of different kinds, as occurred with Iranian dynastic shrines definitely in Commagene and possibly at Shami, Surkh Kotal, Mathura and elsewhere, and at Palmyra with the cult of Baᶜalshamin, who in A.D. 130/1 moved from an abode of Asiatic to one of east Roman design; and the use of the *iwan* as a unit in both religious and secular architecture suggests the same. So it would seem as regards these deities that there was normally no particular connexion between individual cults and types of structure, and that furthermore the architectural forms of a locality could usually satisfy the requirements of those cults present there.

Funerary practices normally demanded some sort of structure for housing the remains of the deceased. This was frequently simple. A pile of stones could suffice in the Syrian desert. The trench was widely popular, reflecting in its precise forms either Iranian, Semitic or Greek traditions. If custom and purse permitted a coffin could be provided, of wood, clay, terracotta or, rarely, stone; in north-east Iran this could take the form of a clay ossuary. Some more elaborate kinds of structure also appeared. An underground tomb or hypogeum was one, usually approached down steps and with a central corridor off which opened recesses or side chambers for sarcophagi; this became common from Susa westwards across Mesopotamia and Syria (Pl. Vc). Others stood above ground as chamber tombs of a variety of types, many of which were created in the Seleucid or Parthian eras. Some continued the old tradition of cave tombs, like those at Edessa and on the Persian Gulf island of Kharg. Some reflected temples, like the Greek Herôon at Aï Khanum or perhaps the early Parthian 'mausoleum' at New Nisa. Many resembled houses in some degree, such as those at Hatra and Assur and also at Syrian Palmyra, where a few boasted an internal colonnaded court. But the most striking by far of all the western Asiatic tombs were the tall towers of Syria, of brick near Dura-Europos but of limestone at Edessa and, most impressively of all, at Palmyra, where they line the ancient ways out of the city (Pl. Vb).

4. 'Parthian' art

The arts of the ancient near east, in their innumerable local and regional manifestations, embodied qualities that remained substantially the same for millennia. Where artists represented the world around them, their approach was strongly conceptual: what they showed only approximated to reality, in a way aesthetically acceptable within their own society. Their work shows a liking for linearity and decorative patternings, as well as for ornamental detail. The subject matter was frequently royal or religious. Art forms and motifs tended to stay in the repertoire over long periods of time, although constantly adapted to changing conditions. Human and animal figures normally appeared in profile. Sculptors working on a plane surface preferred low relief.

The invading Greeks brought with them a profoundly different art. Their artists aimed to produce an aesthetically satisfying approximation to nature, the first such naturalistic style the world had known. In achieving this aim the Greek artists were using preconceived schemas, and setting them within carefully thought out overall designs, just as much as their oriental counterparts. But the difference lay in the result: the elements of the natural world as represented by the artists of the Classical and Hellenistic Greek world look remarkably realistic. Figures could appear in a variety of attitudes, and sculptors could use high relief. This realistic approach, and the rather different repertoire of Greek art, inevitably constituted a challenge to near eastern arts. Admittedly, the oriental world had had a foretaste of what was to come already under Achaemenid rule, when kings and local governors had from time to time employed Greek artists, and thus introduced some slight Hellenization. But not it was Greeks who were dominant throughout western Asia, and the challenge was infinitely greater than it had ever been before.

The results of this cultural clash were complex. For something like three centuries, in the Seleucid and earlier Parthian eras, work was produced in western Asia which varied in style from purely Greek to almost wholly Asiatic, depending on the kind of workshop in which it had been produced. Greek style was used most often for art forms imported from Greece, and near eastern for old Asiatic genres such as rock relief; but much work was produced in mixed styles, such as that of first-century Commagene. From roughly the turn of our era, the Greek element in the styles of this region diminishes; oriental styles reassert themselves, but in forms which show a certain absorption of Hellenism. Because these oriental styles are clearly interrelated, and were employed within the Parthian empire, they have often been collectively labelled as 'Parthian art'. This term is unsatisfactory for many reasons. It implies a stylistic unity which did not exist: styles varied from locality to locality, and from genre to genre. It implies a geographical unity which was also non-existent, for these styles were related to others outside the empire: those of western Parthia are similar to those of desert Syria and shaded off into others of the Hauran and Jordan, while to the east there were further styles similarly connected, such as those of the Kushan realm. It is chronologically misleading, for it is usually employed of art of the later Parthian era only. It is also misleading in that very little of the art of the Parthian empire can be attributed directly to Parthian patronage or execution, and much to non-Parthian Iranians and Semites. Nevertheless, as the term has been in use for decades it is perhaps easiest to continue to use it as a label, provided that there is general realization of its drawbacks.

This 'Parthian' art is clearly derived from earlier near eastern styles, particularly Assyrian and Achaemenid Persian. It shares with them a generally didactic or symbolic purpose, a conceptual approach to representation, a hieraticism, linearity and love of patterning and decorative detail; figure poses look stiff and formal. Much of it was intended for an architectural context, as relief, wall-painting or mosaic, or as sculpture meant to stand against a wall or column. The principal stylistic innovation is a certain rounding of forms, inherited from Hellenism. But if the style owes so much to the earlier near east, this is not the case with iconography. Much of the subject matter was, either directly or indirectly, religious. Not many motifs have survived from Achaemenian or earlier periods, although some, such as the 'snail' hair lock, certain animal poses, and the profile view common for figures until the turn of our era, succeeded in doing so. Instead the repertoire is derived partly from the contemporary oriental world, especially its costumes and hairstyles, and above all from the Hellenistic Greek inheritance, which has made a still larger contribution, everywhere visible, from methods of composition to figure types and poses and innumerable details. A striking iconographical development is the widespread use, between desert Syria and Iran, of a frontal pose for human figures on a plane surface, in relief, painting and elsewhere. This pose had been used only sporadically in earlier arts, but from around the turn of our era it largely ousted others in this area, so much so that whole rows of figures may be so aligned. The purpose of this frontality has been much discussed; its intention may have been to bring the spectator psychologically closer to the subjects of a scene.

5. *Religion in the Parthian empire according to its figured monuments*

Religious subjects could be depicted in a variety of art forms in western Asia during the Seleucid and Parthian periods. These included statuary and figurines, relief sculpture either freestanding above graves (at Palmyra) or attached to buildings, rock faces, plaques, vessels or sarcophagi, miniature reliefs on coins or (at Palmyra) little religious tokens, sketches in pen and ink on rocks, walls or vessels, wall-painting and mosaic. The subject matter consisted primarily of the deities of the Iranian, Semitic, Greek and other communities, together with their worshippers, animals and symbols, and to a lesser degree of mythology and ceremonial. More than one aspect of this repertoire may be combined on one monument. Composition on a plane surface is normally either 'processional', with profile figures, or 'paratactic', with frontal figures set side by side; more complex designs are usually derived from Greek art. We shall examine in turn the aspects of Iranian, Semitic, Greek and alien religions that are revealed in western Asiatic art of the Seleucid and Parthian eras.

The Iranians had long hesitated to show their deities in human form. During the Seleucid and Parthian periods, however, this seems to have become acceptable, and because of the lack of a pre-existing Iranian divine iconographical tradition, borrowings were made from both the rich Greek repertoire and the contemporary world. The only divine representations in the Iranian milieu identifiable with any certainty are the colossal statues and relief figures from Commagene in the mid-first century B.C., accompanied by Greek inscriptions, and the named figures on Kushan coins of the second century A.D. The chief Iranian god Ahura Mazda appears in Commagene as the composite deity Zeus-Oromasdes shown in a somewhat Greek guise as a seated, bearded Zeus with some elements of Iranian costume (Pl. VI). A somewhat similar god with cornucopia standing behind the reclining king in an investiture scene on a rock relief of Tang-i Sarvak, Elymais, west Iran, dating from around A.D. 200, has also been plausibly identified as Ahura Mazda, here perhaps compounded with Semitic Bel through proximity with Babylonia (Pl. XIIc). On coins of the Kushan king Kanishka he is called Mozdooano, wears Iranian dress and rides a unique, two-headed horse. The old god Mithra is named Apollo-Mithras-Helios-Hermes in Commagene, where he is shown beardless, in Iranian-dress and with the nimbus and rays of a sun god behind his head (Pl. VIIa, b), and his labelled images on Kushan coins are similar; he has also been seen plausibly in a similar figure, but bearded, seated in the Tang-i Sarvak relief (Pl. XIIc), and less convincingly on coins of the Indo-Bactrian kings Plato and Hermaeus, in a bearded, cuirassed relief figure on a late Parthian capital from Elymaean Bard-i Nishandeh (Pl. VIIc) and a figure on a plaque from nearby Masjid-i Solaiman. The recently introduced Verethraghna, god of victory, is called Artagnes-Heracles-Ares in Commagene and normally appears as a Greek nude Heracles with club and Nemean lion skin, although as a colossal statue here his dress is more Iranian (Pl. VIIIa, b), and it is in Iranian dress that he is shown on coins of the Kushan king Kanishka; late Parthian relief figures of a nude Heracles from a temple at west Iranian Masjid-i Solaiman (Pl. IX), in an Elymaean rock relief at Shimbâr (Pl. VIIIc) and on a limestone relief in the Foroughi collection have also been plausibly regarded as depictions of him. As for the demonstrably popular Anahita, the only labelled representation of her that survives is an indistinct female bust on a Palmyrene religious token or tessera (Pl. XIXx), but she has been recognized almost certainly in the Athena-like goddess seated beside Mithra (?) in the Tang-i Sarvak relief (Pl. XIIc), less surely in a standing figure on a Bard-i Nishandeh capital (Pl. Xa) and in a chariot goddess from the mid-Parthian period wall-reliefs of central Asian Khaltchayan (Pl. XIVa, B), and still more doubtfully in Asiatic figurines (Pl. Xb); Anahita, too, might possibly underlie the Hera-like goddess who personifies Commagene and bears the unusual epithet 'all-nourishing' (*pantrophos*) in the Commagenian Greek inscriptions (Pl. VIc). A stone-like object of worship depicted among the late Parthian period rock reliefs of Tang-i Sarvak, Elymais, could be a Semitic sacred stone or baetyl, a cult item doubtless imported from its neighbouring Semitic homeland (Pl. Xc).

Of Iranian myth or legend little survives pictorially, although under this heading the Khaltchayan chariot goddess might be included (Pl. XIVa, B), as well as the continuation particularly in Iranian regions of the ancient near eastern theme of animals, especially in combat (Pl. XI), with a horseman attacking a lion or deer on a 'Bactrian' bowl, seals from Nisa and the second rock relief at Tang-i Sarvak (Pl. XIIIc), a man wrestling with an upright lion on a second stupa relief at north Indian Sanchi and also on the second Tang-i Sarvak rock relief (Pl. XIb), and fights between animals on seal impressions at Taxila and Shahr-i Qumis and later on white-glazed bricks at Seleucia on the Tigris. The religious ceremonial shown most frequently in Iran, on monuments from the south-west, was similarly of earlier near eastern origin, but was currently widely depicted also in Semitic areas: this was the casting of incense by a king, prince, priest or worshipper on to a blazing burner set beside him, whether alone, as on reliefs from Bard-i Nishandeh and Masjid-i Solaiman, in front of attendants as on a royal Bard-i Nishandeh relief (Pl. XIIIa), or before a deity—a Heracles figure (that is, Verethraghna?) in the known instances of the late Parthian reliefs at Shimbar (Pl. VIIIc) and in the Foroughi collection. Later Parthian-period monuments from this area also depict the old near eastern religious gesture by mortals of raising the right hand palm forwards in reverence (Pl. Xc). Designs on coin reverses of the vassal kings of Persis illustrate fire worship (Pl. XVIee). The Iranian ceremonial bundle of twigs (*barsom*) is represented only in the Seleucid period, in the hand of a prince on a door-jamb relief at Persepolis and held by priests (?) in the west Iranian rock reliefs of Dukkan-i Daud and Deh-i Nau; one attendant on the late Parthian Bard-i Nishandeh royal sacrifice relief holds an indistinct object, perhaps another cult item (Pl. XIIIa).

Much Iranian religious art of this period was concerned with royalty. Firstly, kings sought to demonstrate divine approval for their régime. This could be done by the portrayal of the investiture of a monarch with the Iranian 'ring of office' by one deity, as in the Commagenian relief from the east terrace of Nemrud Dağ (Pl. XIIa), or by several, as in the late Parthian relief at Tang-i Sarvak where a reclining local king Worôd holds the ring before deities tentatively identified as Ahura Mazda-Bel, Mithra and Anahita (Pl. XIIc). This was also done in Commagene by the commissioning of numerous reliefs of the king shaking hands on equal terms with his divinities (Pls. VIb, VIIb, VIIIb), and of further reliefs of a lion-horoscope, setting Commagenian royalty in an astral context (Pl. XIIb). The Parthian king Gotarzes, by contrast, had himself shown in a rock relief at Bisutun on horseback defeating a horse-riding opponent, with a winged female personification of victory hovering over his own head (Pl. XIIIb). Secondly, kings sought to establish their own dynasty firmly in the eyes of the public, partly through religious references. This could be done through the simple depiction of the dynast and members of his family, whether on coin obverses (Pls. XVI-XVII), in limestone sculptures as in Commagene (Pls. VIb, c, VIIb, VIIIb), in clay reliefs and sculptures as at the central Asian sites of Khaltchayan (Pl. XIVa, B), Dalverzin Tepe and Toprak Kala, on a rock relief as at Tang-i Sarvak (Pl. XIIIc), or in wall-painting as at the late Parthian-period 'palace' of Kuh-i Khwaja in east Iran (Pl. XIVc); the precise religious connotations of such portrayals are obscure. Or the spirits, called *daimones* in the Commagenian inscriptions, of deceased ancestral kings could be made the object of reverence. The monarchs of Commagene were concerned to trace their ancestry to the Achaemenid Darius I and to Alexander the Great, and selected figures from this family tree, in appropriate costumes were included among the reliefs at the mountain shrine of Nemrud Daǧ (Pl. XVa). Other sanctuaries in the Iranian world may also have been devoted to royal ancestral cults, such as that at Shami in west Iran (Pl. XVb) and later the Kushan shrines of Afghan Surkh Kotal (Pl. XVc) and north Indian Mathura (Pl. XVd) with their inscriptions and shattered princely statuary. It has further been suggested that the profile archer holding a bow on the reverse of numerous Parthian royal coins, shown seated first on a four-legged stool and later on an omphalos or throne, similarly represents the divinized founder of the Arsacid dynasty, Arshak or Arsaces (Pl. XVIhh, kk, yy). Thirdly, kings tried to maintain their authority by appointing vassals or officials, and south-west Iranian reliefs not infrequently appear to portray either such investitures or at least the payment of homage by one or more subordinates: the senior figure may ride on horseback, as in the rock reliefs of Hung-i Nauruzi (Pl. XVIIIa) and Sar-i Zohab, stand, as do Mithradates II in his rock relief at Bisutun (Pl. XVIIIb) and a diadem-holding figure in the rock relief of Hong-e Yar-ᶜAliwand (a scene also perhaps visible in stucco relief at Kuh-i Khwaja), or sit, as does the Parthian king Artabanus V while investing Khwasak, satrap of Susa, with the ring of office on a lamentably executed stele dated 14 September, A.D. 215 (Pl. XVIIIc). Fourthly, the high rank of the senior person present in a scene could be emphasized in west Iranian monuments by showing subordinate figures making one of two gestures of respect, either the old oriental one of holding up the right hand palm-forwards (Pl. XVIIIa), or the folding of arms, a gesture apparently depicted only in Elymais (Pl. XIIIa, c).

Lastly, it is possible that the relief of a man reclining at a funerary banquet, carved on the rear interior wall of a late Parthian-period rock tomb on the Persian Gulf island of Kharg, gives a glimpse into Iranian funerary beliefs; but as this theme is otherwise unknown in the Iranian world and is widespread in Semitic regions, and as furthermore Kharg was on the sea route from Semitic Mesopotamia to India, it is equally possible that the monument is a Semitic intrusion.

The Semites themselves had no inhibitions about the representation of their own objects of worship, whether anthropomorphic deities, animals or symbolic inanimate items, for among many of their communities there were traditions for such portrayals that were already millennia old. This practice continued to flourish, particularly in the later Parthian period. Inscriptions, commonly in Aramaic, often identify buildings and objects, and are frequently dated, usually according to the Seleucid era. The iconographical repertoire is drawn mainly from Hellenistic Greek and contemporary Semitic and Iranian sources, with lesser contributions from the earlier near east or Rome. Surviving representations of objects of worship and attendant figures become frequent especially from around the turn of our era onwards, in the area of Mesopotamia and desert Syria; they most commonly take the form of limestone reliefs or plaques attached to buildings, less often of statuary in the round, figurines, altar reliefs, terracotta relief tokens (*tesserae*), wall-paintings or portrayals in other genres. The Semitic repertoire is marked by a considerable iconographical fluidity; one deity may appear under a number of differing guises or be abbreviated to a bust, head or hand, and identification is often difficult without an accompanying text.

The figures of an anthropomorphic gods form an important part of this repertoire. Gods may wear civilian dress, in which case their divine status is usually indicated by special attributes such as the Greek sceptre or cylindrical headdress (polos) (Pls. XIXc, y, XX, XXI, XXVIIb), and often by a smooth nimbus or rays around the head to indicate a celestial function. The items of costume may be variously drawn from the Greek sleeveless tunic, cloak and sandals (e.g. Pl. XXIa), Aramaic or Arab tunics, cloaks and 'skirts' (Pls. XIXt, XXVc, XXVIIIa, b), or Parthian sleeved tunic, trousers and shoes (e.g. Pl. XXXIa), depending on area and deity. Often, however, the gods were militarized, perhaps to improve their protective capacities. They might carry a lance or other military equipment (e.g. Pl. XXVIII), or wear a full cuirass (e.g. Pl. XXVII), an item which is reserved for divinities alone in art and is usually of Hellenistic Greek shape, although Roman types infiltrated Palmyra and Dura-Europos from the second century A.D. onwards. Often this cuirass is shown being worn over a Parthian tunic and trousers (e.g. Pl. XXVII). The gods are most frequently portrayed standing normally at ground level, but occasionally on the back of an animal (Pl. XXXIIIc) or in a chariot (Pl. XXVIIIc); less commonly they sit, recline, or ride a horse (Pl. XXVIIIa, b), dromedary (Pls. XIXm, XXXIVc) or other appropriate beast. The representations of named individual gods illustrate the considerable fluidity of this repertoire. Thus the supreme god Bel, in his named and probable appearences at Palmyra, is always beardless and cuirassed, but his headdress, normally a *polos*, is sometimes changed to a diadem on tesserae (Pls. XIX-XXI); of his two probable depictions in the wall-paintings of the Temple of Bel at Dura-Europos, the later shows him cuirassed again (Pl. XXII), but the earlier of *c.* A.D. 50, although mostly gone, preserves a lower leg and foot in Parthian costume which suggests that here his whole figure may originally have been in Parthian dress. Baʿalshamin, both at Dura-Europos and Palmyra, is shown in civilian tunic and cloak and seated in named representations (Pl. XXIVa), but he has also been recognized, not necessarily correctly, in an unnamed, standing cuirassed god at Palmyra (Pl. XXIVb). Other leading Semitic deities were similarly treated. Nebû appears in labelled manifestations at Palmyra and Dura-Europos either as a nude Apollo (Pl. XIXa) or in a long tunic and cloak (Pls. XIXbb, XXIVc), often clasping Apollo's lyre. A nude Heracles figure from the north Gate at Hatra was labelled Nergal, so the numerous Heracles figures found in Semitic regions at Hatra, Dura-Europos, Palmyra and elsewhere doubtless in fact represent this Babylonian deity (Pls. XXVa, b, XXXVIIIb). The Arab sun god Shamash is pictured as a radiate bust both on a Palmyrene tessera (Pl. XIXp) and on a relief from the back wall of Building A at Hatra, where he is called Marên, 'Our Lord' and is horned and diademed (Pl. XXVIa, cf. XXVIb); another Palmyrene tessera has the frontal helmeted head of a lesser known Arab deity, Shai al-Qaum. Several west Semitic deities are pictured in our area only at Palmyra, like the bearded and normally cuirassed healing deity Shadrafa, usually accompanied on reliefs and tesseras by a snake and scorpion (Pl. XXVIIa, XXXVIIIb); tesserae also portray the dead Tammuz lying on a bed and the beardless busts of Elqonera (cf. Pl. XXXVIIIb) and Belhammon. Of the more local Semitic deities, three Palmyrene gods are portrayed both at Palmyra and Dura-Europos: Iarhibôl normally stands cuirassed with a solar radiate halo round his head (Pls. XXb, c, XXIb), ʿAglibôl is marked by a lunar crescent over or later behind his head and exchanges civilian dress for a military cuirass in the first century A.D. (Pls. XX, XXI, XXIVb, XXVa, XXXVIIIa, c), and Malakbel has two aspects throughout, wearing either civilian dress (Pls. XXVa, XXVIIc) or a cuirass with a radiate nimbus behind his head (Pls. XXa, XXIa, XXIVb, XXVIIc, XXXVIII), doubtless corresponding respectively to his vegetation and solar natures. The god Aphlad is shown at Dura wearing a cuirass over Parthian tunic and trousers (Pl. XXVIIb). Arab deities such as Abgal (Pl. XXVIIIb), Arsû and his associate ʿAzîzû, Asherû (or Ashar) and his companion Saʿar (of Saʿad, Pl. XXVIIIa), and the guardian spirits (*ginnayê*, genii) of places are normally pictured in the Palmyrene area and at Dura-Europos in local tunic, cloak and 'skirt', sometimes mounted on horse (Pl. XXVIIIa, b) or dromedary (Pl. XXXIVc); but Arsû (like the similar Arsûbel on a Palmyrene tessera) may also be cuirassed (Pls. XIXk, XXb, c, XXIa, cf. XXXVIIIb), and a god, in a relief dated A.D. 263, wears Persian dress (Pl. XXVIIIc). Representations of the Gad or personified Fortune of a place vary still more: those of localities around Palmyra, seen on Palmyrene tesserae, are of several kinds, that of Palmyra itself, shown in relief and painting at Dura-Europos, is a female resembling the famous Hellenistic Greek seated personification of the Tyche of Antioch (Pls. XXIII, XXIXb), while that of Dura-Europos, represented in association with Palmyra, changes from a Baʿalshamin-like seated male in A.D. 159 (Pl. XXIXa) to a Tyche-like female *c.* A.D. 239 (Pl. XXIII). At Hatra the 'Son of Our Lord' (Bar-Marên) resembles his father Marên (Shamash) on a relief bust from Building A but with crescent added (Pl. XXXa), while a bronze mask found in front of the great temple labelled 'for Bar-Marên' in fact represents the Greek Dionysus, suggesting identification (Pl. XXXb). Of the numerous unnamed representations of gods, doubtless many are further portrayals of these named deities, while others picture deities not mentioned at all in written texts. The figure types, and extent of militarization, correspond particularly closely between Dura-Europos and Palmyra, and the cuirass reappears on a god on a late Parthian period stele from Characene. At Hatra, however, few deities are named in accompanying texts, and figure types tend to differ somewhat: gods often wear local garments (Pl. XXVc, XXXIIa), and although many carry weapons like their Syrian counterparts (Pl. XXVc), the cuirass is represented on only one figure, which is unnamed and usually identified as Aššurbel but more likely portrays the Apollo of Syrian Hierapolis and is therefore a Syrian intrusion (Pl. XXXc). Other divine identities are also puzzling: is the bearded axe-holding god accompanied by a three-headed dog on a Hatrene relief Nergal again or Hadad, a god not mentioned in known Hatrene texts (Pl. XXXIa), and is

Hadad to be recognized on another Hatrene relief of a god seated holding a double axe and thunderbolt, as he surely is in Durene and north Syrian reliefs of the chief deities of Hierapolis (Pl. XXXIb)? And what is the snake-legged monster, recalling Greek giant and Scylla figures, visible on a Palmyrene Bel temple relief of *c.* A.D. 32 (Pl. XXXVIIIb)?

Goddess figures present similar problems, but are fewer and less varied. Most look Greek. The largest group portrays the subject in Greek ankle-length tunic (chiton) and long cloak (himation), often with lance or sceptre, sometimes with diadem or polos (Pls. XXI, XXVa, XXXI, XXXII). To these belong the named representations of Ishtar, Beltî, Astarte (Pls. XXa, XXIa), and Manôt on Palmyrene reliefs and tesserae, as well as the Tyche-like Gads of Palmyra and Dura-Europos depicted in Durene relief and wall-painting (Pls. XXIII, XXIXb), and the relief bust of Martên (accompanied by bearded snakes) from Building A at Hatra (Pl. XXXIIb). Nanai and Ishtarbad, named on Palmyrene tesserae, have the traits of Greek Artemis (Pl. XIXv, cf. XXXVIIIb). The great Arab goddess Allat, whose labelled figure often occurs in Palmyrene relief and tesserae, appears during the first century A.D. in civilian dress (Pl. XXXIIIa) but is later given the traits of the armed and helmeted Athena (Pl. XXXIIIb), and doubtless Allat should also be seen in the unnamed Athena figures of Palmyra, Dura-Europos and Hatra (Pl. XXXIIIc). The greatest goddess of whom there is as yet no labelled image is Atargatis, although she may be recognized almost certainly as the figure in civilian dress, often seated and wearing a polos, in the Durene and north Syrian Hierapolis deities reliefs (Pl. XXXIb), in the Hatrene relief of a god and three-headed dog (Pl. XXXIa) and less surely in other figures at Hatra, Dura-Europos and Palmyra.

Other characteristic Semitic objects of worship are also shown. The religious standard, called *semeion* by the Roman writer Lucian (*De Syria Dea*, 33), occurs frequently, hung with often astral symbols and ever changing in its forms (Pl. XXXI, XXXIVa). Two and three sacred stones or baetyls respectively are pictured on two Palmyrene tesserae (Pl. XIXe), and others may be shown being carried in procession on a Palmyra Bel temple beam relief (Pl. XXXIXb), and being worshipped on the second rock relief at west Iranian Tang-i Sarvak (Pls. Xc, XIIIc), where this would constitute a Semitic intrusion. The trees depicted on a Bel temple beam relief and on tesserae at Palmyra are also probably sacred (Pl. XXXVIIIa). Various creatures from the animal kingdom are pictured in religious contexts, usually doubtless as attributes of the deities, but sometimes perhaps as objects of worship in themselves. Common throughout the region are subjects already popular in the ancient near east, the fabulous griffin (Pls. XXVIIc, XXVIIIc), the lion (Pls. XXXIIIc, XXXIVb), bull (Pl. XXVIIIc), horse (Pls. XXVIIIa, b, XXXVIIIb), goat (Pl. XXXVIIIa), snake (Pls. XXVIIa, XXVIIIb, XXXIa, XXXIIb), scorpion (Pls. XXVIIa, XXXIa), and the eagle, symbolic of cosmic deities (Pls. XXVIIc, XXXc, XXXVIIIc), which is addressed as 'Our Lord, the eagle' and depicted alone on reliefs and local coins at Hatra (Pl. XXXIVa) The fish (Pl. XXXVIIIb), deer, donkey (Pl. XXXIXb) and dog (Pl. XXXIa, XXXVIIIb) occur in various contexts; the sheep is sometimes carried in the arms of worshippers (Pl. XXIVa: it also appears with Christ (Pl. XLVIIc), and on the Torah shrine (Pl. XLVIII), in Durene murals). The dromedary is portrayed on Syrian reliefs, Palmyrene tesserae and the terracottas of Seleucia on the Tigris, usually as a divine mount (Pl. XXXIVc). The dove (of Atargatis?) is current at

Palmyra and Dura-Europos, and a weird human-headed cock occupies a Palmyrene tessera.

Also reverenced, as inscriptions make clear, were the objects in which the souls of deceased mortals were believed to reside, their *nefesh*, generally carefully labelled. These could be a simple stone or plaque, but some took on elaborate artistic forms imported from the Greek and Roman west but locally interpreted, most notably at Palmyra. The earliest was the large or small stele at Assur (Pl. XXXVa) or Palmyra with a full-length figure of the deceased, soon followed at Palmyra early in the first century A.D. by the funerary statue; from *c.* A.D. 50, however, the popular funerary relief bust proliferated, especially at Palmyra, adapted from a metropolitan Roman model and used at Palmyra to close off the end of a burial compartment within a tomb (Pl. XXXVb). Later, a painted bust (Pl. XXXVI), or a figure shown attending a funerary banquet (Pl. XXXVc), could serve as alternatives. It has been suggested that, at Palmyra at least, the term *nefesh* lost its earlier significance, and came simply to denote a funerary monument. Further light may be thrown on funerary beliefs by the figured decoration added to some Parthian-period terracotta sarcophagi from Mesopotamia: nude (?) females (goddesses?) within aediculae from the north (Pl. XXXVIIa), and half-females or soldiers from the south (Pl. XXXVIIb).

Concerning the theology, myths and legends of the Semitic cults the compositions into which these figures and items were set provide some hints. Deities are frequently placed side by side, in groups of up to eight. Their identities and positioning often seem to illustrate the astral theology of Hellenistic Babylonia. Thus male pairs are common, and may sometimes symbolize the morning and evening stars (Pls. XIXaa, XXVIIIa, b). Triads are recognizable: that of Our Lord (Shamash), Our Lady and the Son of Our Lord at Hatra (Pls. XXVI, XXXa, b, XXXIIb), and that of the supreme god Bel, the solar Iarhibôl and the lunar ʿAglibôl at Palmyra, are documented in texts and art (Pls. XX, XXI), while Palmyrene religious reliefs may also suggest the existence there of a second triad, that of Baʿalshamin, the lunar ʿAglibôl and Malakbel in his solar aspect (Pl. XXIVb). Glimpses of complex myths perhaps occur in some of the Palmyrene temple reliefs of *c.* A.D. 32, where ʿAglibôl and Malakbel shake hands over an altar between a temple and a sacred tree (Pl. XXXVIIIa), and elsewhere a row of deities is engaged in battle with a snake-legged giant (Pl. XXXVIIIb), a scene paralleled in abbreviated form on a Roman-period lintel from Soueida in south Syria; a Palmyrene religious relief pictures a god holding lions on chains. Ancient near eastern themes recur in the Palmyrene religious lintel (and Hatrene pediment) dominated by an eagle with outspread wings (Pl. XXXVIIIC) and scenes of animals in procession on early Palmyrene reliefs, and in combat at Palmyra, Dura-Europos and Seleucia on the Tigris.

Certain Semitic religious practices are also illustrated. The commonest is that pictured since ancient near eastern days, the casting of incense on to a flaming burner by a royal, priestly or civilian worshipper, often before one or more deities usually represented on the other side of the burner (Pls. XXII, XXIII, XXVIIIb, XXIXb, XXXIXa); sometimes an incense box or bowl is held (Pl. XXIXb). Occasionally a second worshipper is shown as in attendance (Pl. XXVIIIc). Religious processions also feature: early Palmyrene reliefs show profile men and women carrying offerings, reliefs from the Palmyrene temples of Bel and Allat picture processions involving ritually veiled women and a dromedary (Pl.

XXXIXb), and a damaged relief from Dura-Europos may also have shown a dromedary procession. One Hatrene temple relief presents the busts of musicians, and another portrays the local king Sanatruq and an architect presenting a model temple to a seated goddess. Two gestures are commonly made: the old near eastern raising of the right hand palm forwards, which when performed by deities probably indicates benediction (Pls. XXVIIIb, XXXIIIa), and when by mortals probably adoration (Pl. XXXIXb), and the doubtless Semitic raising of both hands palm-forwards, signifying prayer, invocation or supplication (Pl. XXXIXc). Priests were often distinguished by their dress, sometimes by tunics that were longer or by waistbands that were wider than the norm, and habitually by tall headdresses, the cylindrical and frequently wreathed *modius* at Palmyra perhaps worn over a skullcap (Pls. XIXl, s, XXIX), or the conical variety seen more at Dura-Europos (Pls. XXVIIb, XXXIXa) and in south Syria. Attendants carry bowls, amphorae, ladles, drinking horns (rhytons) and other equipment. The tesserae of Palmyra, normally issued as tokens for entry to cult banquets or for participation in a religious distribution of foodstuffs, picture these and further cult items, the sacred couches of Bel, Astarte and of the priests, pointed vases, wine-mixing bowls (craters) and possibly a ritual mask (Pl. XIXb). Palmyrene monuments, in particular, also illuminate funerary practices, frequently portraying funerary banquets (Pl. XXXVc) and sometimes showing women with hair dishevelled and with their bared breasts marked by groups of gashes in the old Semitic mourning ritual (Pl. XXXVb).

Greek art had an enormous impact. To depict individual deities, the Greeks normally used the anthropomorphic figure types imported from their homeland; characteristic attributes often assisted identification. Greek figure types, however, were often used syncretistically to represent Asiatic divinities, as has been seen, so whenever a Greek figure type appears, it should be questioned whether it is depicting a Greek or oriental deity.

The range of male divinities was wide. Among the most popular figures was that of the chief god Zeus, normally bearded and cloaked and often bare-torsoed, frequently standing, frequently seated, often holding a sceptre, an eagle or a personified Victory (Nike), and appearing on numerous Greek and Iranian coin reverses, (Pls. XVIcc, XVIIhh, r, ss), as Seleucid-period statuary at Aï Khanum, Afghanistan and Nihavand, Iran (Pl. XLa), as Commagenian Zeus-Oromasdes (Pl. VI) and later in Palmyrene and Durene relief (Pl. XXIVa) and on a circular ivory disc from Hatra with other Olympian deities (Pl. XLb). Still more popular was the figure of Heracles, usually nude and distinguished by carrying his club and the skin of the Nemean lion he had vanquished, normally standing but occasionally fighting, drunk, resting or reclining (*cubans*). Heracles figures frequently appeared on Seleucid (Pl. XVIc) and later western Asiatic coins, including Parthian issues (Pl. XVIjj) and one of the Kushan king Huvishka (labelled Erakilo). Before the turn of our era were also shown standing on a Susa terracotta, on an ivory rhyton from early Parthian Nisa (where Heracles' club also appeared as architectural decoration in the 'Round Hall', Pl. XLIa), and on Commagenian monuments (Pl. VIIIa, b), reclining on a Seleucid rock relief at Bisutun dated June, 148 B.C. (Pl. XLIb), and drunk on a pot fragment from Peshawar, Pakistan. Later, his figures were even more widespread in the same poses, except that where he fights the Nemean lion this is in a attitude more ancient near eastern than classical. These figures appear on reliefs (Pls. XXVa, XXXVIIIb) and tesserae (Pl. XIXi) at Palmyra, in over forty depictions in statuary and relief at Dura-

Europos, in numerous examples of statuary (Pl. XXVb) and relief at Hatra (where he is once shown fighting a Centaur, Pl. XLIc), at Assur, in statuary and relief at Masjid-i Solaiman (Pl. IX) and standing, diademed, in the Shimbar rock relief (Pl. VIIIc), and on a Kushan terracotta from Bactra and a Kushan relief from north Indian Mathura. Figures of Dionysus with his special staff (thyrsus), grapes and panther as attributes (Pl. XIXj, XXXb), of Apollo with his lyre (Pls. XIXi, XLIIa), and of the radiate sun god Helios are almost as widespread in area and genre, but less frequently shown. The figure of Eros as a nude, winged boy is extremely popular, occurring first as a silver statuette and ivory rhyton relief figure at Nisa (Pl. XLIIIa) and on figurines from Seleucia on the Tigris, and in the mid-Parthian period on Parthian coins, Seleucia terracottas, holding up garlands on clay frieze at Khaltchayan, on Taxila terracottas and a toilet tray from near Peshawar; later it is found across the region, from Palmyrene relief, Durene wall-painting and stucco, imported Hatrene statuary, a Seleucia ivory box relief and bronze figurine from Nihavand to more easterly areas, as a horse-riding figure on a painted coffer of a vaulted ceiling at east Iranian Kuh-i Khwaja, as an imported statuette and plaster medallion at Afghan Begram, and finally holding up garlands in relief on buildings at Surkh Kotal (Pl. XLIIb) and Taxila and on a Kanishka reliquary from Peshawar. Other divine figures were less popular. That of Poseidon was found on an imported plaster case at Hellenistic Aï Khanum and on coin reverses of the Indo-Bactrians and of the Indo-Parthian Gondophares; later his figure occurs perhaps on a Palmyrene relief (Pl. XXXVIIIb), on a Hatrene ivory relief (Pl. XLb), in an east Roman marble statue found outside Hatrene temple E ('of Marên'), and perhaps in the trident-carrying figure (identified with Iranian Verethraghna, or Hindu Śiva?) of the wall-paintings of Kuh-i Khwaja (Pl. XLIIc) and of the coins of the Kushan Kadphises. Hermes appears first on eastern Seleucid coins, like the Dioscuri, and later in statuary and relief at Nineveh (Pl. XLIIIb), Hatra, and Palmyra, where in the Bel temple his bust represents the planet Mercury, alongside Ares as Mars, and Saturn (Pl. XLIVa). A standing Harpocrates is featured during the first two centuries A.D. in a north Mesopotamian terracotta and imported bronze figurines at Begram and Taxila. Of the lesser and more grotesque male divinities, centaurs are pictured at early Parthian Nisa as a figurine and as rhyton-ends (replacing older oriental monsters in this position), on mid-Parthian gems from Merv, and finally in a 'cultbank' relief from Hatra (Pl. XLIc). Silenus is portrayed on Seleucid stone bowl fragments from Denavar (Pl. XLIIIc) and a Gandharan frieze, while satyr heads are seen on a Nisa imported marble statuette, in the stucco decoration of around the turn of our era on the Apsidal Temple of Taxila, and later on a Roman-period stucco house cornice at Dura-Europos. Tritons are shown on coins of the Indo-Bactrian Hippostratus, and much later in reliefs from Edessa and, like Atlas, from Gandharan buildings. Ithyphallic Priapus occurs once, in Palmyrene relief.

The variety of Greek goddess figures is almost as great. Victory, personified as winged Nike often holding a wreath, is ubiquitous, in statuary, relief (Pls. XIa, L, XIIIb, XLIVb), coins (Pl. XVIo, pp) and wall-painting (Pl. XXXVI), from Syria to Gandhara throughout the Seleucid and Parthian eras; and helmeted Athena figures with aegis and spear are only a little less widespread (Pls. XVIImm, uu, XXXIIIb, c). Fortune, personified as Tyche with her mural crown, standing or sometimes seated in the attitude of the statue of the Tyche of Antioch, is also commonly seen on Seleucid, Parthian (Pl.

XVIqq, vv), Indo-Bactrian and Indo-Scythian coin reverses, on Nisa seal impressions, and later in relief and wall-painting at Hatra, Dura-Europos (Pls. XXIII, XXIXb) and Palmyra, as well, perhaps, in a marble head from Susa. Aphrodite, usually half-clad or nude, is portrayed on Seleucia terracottas and a toilet tray from near Peshawar, in imported marble statuary at Nisa, Shami and later Hatra, in a statue fragment, plaster plaques and a house mural at Dura-Europos, and as a relief bust on the Palmyrene Bel temple north thalamos planetary ceiling, where she represents Venus and unexpectedly wears a Syrian veil (Pl. XLIVa). Artemis' figure with her bow, quiver and arrows appears on east Seleucid, Bactrian, Indo-Scythian and Parthian coin reverses, on metal plaques and a bowl from central Asia, and seemingly at Palmyra in the Bel temple 'battle' beam relief (Pl. XXXVIIIb) and on tesserae (Pl. XIXv). Medusa and Gorgon heads are seen on some east Seleucid and Bactrian coins, on a terracotta cup medallion from Aï Khanum, and later at Hatra as a bronze mask, on the back of the 'Aššur-Bel' statue (Pl. XXXc), and as architectural decoration on the central iwan temples. Of the less popular goddesses, Hestia and the Muses are visible only on early Parthian period ivory rhyton friezes from Nisa (Pl. XLIIIa), while Demeter and Hekate have been recognized on Indo-Bactrian, and Dikaiosyne (Justice) on Parthian coin reverses. A winged Siren is portrayed in a silver gilt figurine from early Parthian Nisa, and on a Palmyrene funerary relief of the third century A.D. The sphinx was an Iranian preference, present as a figurine at Nisa, as a carved gem subject at Merv, and later as a glazed vase at Begram and a capital at Masjid-i Solaiman, where two sphinxes are set back to back in imitation of Achaemenian animal protome capitals. Latecomers into the repertoire, seen only from the second century A.D. onwards, were Hera, shown with other Olympian deities on a Hatrene ivory disco (Pl. XLb), Leto, dressed in local costume on a Palmyrene relief (Pl. XLIIa), and Nemesis with her fateful wheel, depicted on Palmyrene reliefs (Pl. XXIa) and tesserae (Pl. XIXw) and a Durene relief of A.D. 228/9.

Other items were also supplied by the Greek religious repertoire. Various creatures were often associated with deities. Such were Zeus' eagle (Pls. XVIcc, XXXVIIIc), the owl seen on Indo-Bactrian coin reverses, Apollo's crow on a relief (Pl. XLIIa) and tesserae from Palmyra, the cock, peacock and fabulous gryllos also at Palmyra, the goose on a plaque from Seleucia on the Tigris, and the phoenix, symbolic of rebirth, on a funerary mosaic of Edessa (Pl. XLVa). Such were Heracles' lionskin (Pls. XVIc, jj, XXVa, XXXVIIIb), the common lion-head architectural ornament, ox-heads, some horse representations (notably at Palmyra) with western harnesses, the widespread dog, the antelopes, rabbits and boars of Palmyra and Dura-Europos, Aphrodite's dolphin and the zodiacal crab at Palmyra, and the fabled Pegasus, centaur (Pl. XLIc), chimaera, hippocamp and sphinx. Inanimate attributes included Zeus' thunderbolt (both winged and wingless), Poseidon's trident, Dionysus' thyrsus, Hermes' bag and staff, Eros' torches, Saturn's sickle, Artemis' bow, quiver and arrows, Nemesis' wheel and tiller, and the cornucopia, balance, mirror and Hellenized form of the sceptre. From the western repertoire of the Roman period came the Evil Eye, seen in painting at Palmyra (Pl. XLIVc) and in relief on Temple E at Hatra and a bronze plaque from Masjid-i Solaiman.

Greek mythology and legend were widely illustrated through this repertoire. From the contexts of these scenes, it would seem that they were used in several different ways: most commonly as simple portrayals of the deities concerned, but not infrequently as illustra-

tions of literature, and sometimes as dynastic or funerary symbolism. Simple depiction
was doubtless the purpose of many of the representations that show one deity alone, and of
some, such as certain Nisa rhyton friezes (Pl. XLIIIa) or the circular ivory disc from
Hatra (Pl. XLb), that portray them in groups. To this category also surely belong the examples of the 'inhabited scroll', of Hellenistic Greek origin, a vegetation spiral usually of
acanthus or vines with little figures such as Eros and Pan and animals cavorting within
each spiral: at Palmyra it is to be seen on the soffits of Bel temple beams carved *c.* A.D. 32
(Pl. XLVb) and later as architectural and textile ornament, at Hatra as ornament on a
noble's drapery, and further east in the mid-Parthian period on a metal bowl from
Bokhara and an Indian ivory relief found at Begram. The zodiac, in its late Hellenistic
form, was simply depicted on the Palmyrene Bel temple north thalamos ceiling (Pl.
XLIVa), a Dura-Europos Mithraeum relief of A.D. 170 (Pl. XLVIIb) and probably a
Hatra wall graffito, but in a damaged Palmyrene relief was arranged so as to give an individual's horoscope. Illustration of literature was clearly the purpose of some scenes on
'Bactrian' metal relief bowls from central Asia (Pl. XLVc), where incidents from plays of
Euripides have been recognized, and also of scenes from the Trojan war visible perhaps on
a early Hellenistic plaster cast from Bactrian Aï Khanum, in a Kushan period relief of the
wooden horse from Charsada, and in paintings of the wooden horse and the fall of Troy on
a Roman period wooden parade shield from Dura-Europos; it could also have been the intention of the Babylon terracotta with Europa on the bull, of the Chârsada cosmetic pot
relief of Apollo and Daphne, and of the Durene painted shield with a battle between
Greeks and Amazons. Dynastic symbolism seemingly arose through the close association
between the cult of the Hellenistic kings and that of the twelve leading Olympian gods, the
Dodecatheoi, a slightly fluctuating group which comprised Zeus, Hera, Poseidon,
Demeter, Apollo, Artemis, Ares, Aphrodite, Hermes, Athena, Hephaistos and Hestia in
Eudoxos' canonical list; hence the appearences of many of these deities on coins (Pls.
XVIcc, XVIIhh, mm, r, ss, uu), on Hellenistic plaster casts at Aï Khanum, and on some
early Parthian Nisa ivory rhyton friezes (Pl. XLIIIa), which represent a transference of
this Hellenistic royal ideology to a Parthian context. Greek cults of city founders lived on,
as with that of king Seleucus Nicator at Dura-Europos, recorded in relief (Pl. XXIXa).
Funerary symbolism of the Roman kind is probably intended in the Greek mythological
figures in Syrian funerary art, with (at Palmyra) Arimasps and Meleager hinting at the
struggles of this life in preparation for the next, Achilles on Scyros at the casting off of a
poor existence for a better (Pl. XXXVI), the rape of Ganymede at the rise of the soul to
heaven (Pl. XXXVI), Nikai at victory over death (Pl. XXXVI), and (at Edessa) the
phoenix at rebirth (Pl. XLVa) and Orpheus at bliss in paradise. Lastly, it is possible that
Hellenistic votive scenes underlie the Palmyrene Bel temple 'Sanctuary' relief despite its
oriental content (Pl. XXXVIIIa).

   Greek religious ritual is not much portrayed. The scene of the casting of incense on to a
burner, although adopted in the Greek and Roman worlds, was originally near eastern,
and its survival in the Parthian period and area was doubtless due more to near eastern
than to western inspiration, as we have seen. The genuinely Greek libation is pictured on
a 'Bactrian' bowl (Pl. XLVc) and an imported plaster medallion from Begram. Crowning
with a laurel wreath is also represented, both by one deity of another, by a mortal of a deity, and by a deity of mortal (Pls. XVIo, XLIVb) in the later Parthian period. The holding

of a sheep by a youth is pictured from A.D. 31 onwards at Palmyra and at Dura-Europos (Pl. XXIVa: here Christ carries a huge sheep across his shoulders in the Baptistry frescoes of c. A.D. 240, Pl. XLVIIc). As for funerary ceremonial, the funerary banquet scene, often illustrated, has been borrowed from Hellenistic antecedents but much adapted (Pl. XXXVc). Gestures such as the resting of the fingers against the cheek (in sorrow?) by women and children, the holding of the veil by women in certain ways, or the proffering of items by servants, have been inherited from Greek funerary art, but how far they represent ritual is problematic; similarly with the laying of a comforting hand on the shoulder, common in Roman Republican and Augustan funerary sculpture.

From outside the Iranian world, alien religions impinged. To the east were those of India. From the second century B.C., following the establishment of the Indo-Greek (or 'Indo-Bactrian') kingdoms and perhaps partly inspired by their anthropomorphic divine figures, north Indian representative arts, and especially sculpture, blossomed, with numerous figures and reliefs adorning religious buildings. Hindu gods were portrayed: frontal figures of Indra and the solar Surya in a four-horse chariot decorated buildings, sometimes in association with Buddhist figures and symbols (indicating religious conflation), the first known depictions of Vishnu and Śiva appeared on a drachm of the early Indo-Bactrian monarch Agathocles, whose coins showed a dancing girl (Yakshî?), and associated animals appeared (Pl. XVIIk, kk, l, ll). A second blossoming followed under the Kushans, particularly Kanishka, with the often frontal figures of these and other deities such as Brahma and Hariti present, but frequently certain of them, such as Indra and Brahma, accompanying the Buddha, again through conflation (Pl. XLVIa). Perhaps it is three of these Hindu gods, including Śiva, who were grouped in a wall-painting of the east Iranian Kushan-period 'palace' of Kuh-i Khwaja (Pl. XLIIc). The Buddhist artistic repertoire was also developing from well before the turn of our era at Bharhut, Sanchi and elsewhere, with scenes from the Buddha's life and of the veneration of the Buddha's headdress in the paradise of the Hindu god Indra, through conflation. But as yet the Buddha's presence was indicated only by symbols such as his footprint, headdress or empty throne. Buddhist art flowered enormously under Kushan patronage, and its repertoire developed (Pl. XLVIb, c): most importantly from the time of king Kanishka the Buddha himself could be portrayed anthropomorphically, even on coins (Pl. XVIIxx), appearing as a somewhat Apollo-like figure in long robes (Pl. XLVIa). Some consider that this change arose through internal developments in Buddhism, others, perhaps with more reason, that it formed part of Kanishka's political policy of encouraging all religions within his empire and depicting all their deities on monuments, in the anthropomorphic manner that was at least partly a western inheritance in the region. Now the Buddha was commonly shown surrounded by his archangels, the Boddhisattva. Other aspects of Indian religion are illuminated by the seven Andhra dynastic royal portraits carved in a shrine at Nanaghat, doubtless under the inspiration of Hellenistic Greek and Iranian dynastic art, and by the frequent artistic occurrence of the *mithuna*, the erotic couple symbolizing fruitful union.

From the west, other religions intruded. From Egypt came the worship of Isis, exemplified in an imported bronze early Hellenistic figurine of the goddess found at Nihavand in west Iran. From Anatolia came those of Cybele, portrayed with two of her eunuch priests on a silver gilded medallion of c. 300 B.C. discovered at Bactrian Aï Khanum, of the Attis-like figures on the Bel temple peristyle ceiling and in a tomb painting of Palmyra, and perhaps of the torch-carrying 'dadaophoroi' in Anatolian dress on a Palmyrene tessera. From Rome came the legend of the twins Romulus and Remus being suckled by a she-wolf, illustrated on a battered relief found in the Palmyrene temple of Bel; and the curious discovery at Hatra of what could have been a local portrait head of Trajan might hing at an awareneas of the Roman imperial cult (Pl. XLVIIa). But most significant were three great religions that came to Dura-Europos and left important monuments executed in the local artistic styles under Roman occupation (*c.* A.D. 165-256). The first was the Roman cult of Mithraism, with a Mithraeum dedicated by Palmyrene mounted archers; here coloured limestone reliefs dated A.D. 168 and 170 illustrate Mithras' slaughter of the bull (Pl. XLVIIb), and wall-paintings of *c.* A.D. 211-216 portray this and other events in Mithras' life, including him hunting, as well as the two Mithraic prophets and a scene of the initiation of the Sun into his cult, in compositions which seem to correspond well with other Mithraic scenes from elsewhere in the Roman empire. Next to leave traces was Judaism: in the earlier third century A.D. a house was converted into a Jewish synagogue, and the walls were decorated with panelled and floral motifs; but in or after A.D. 244/5 the House of Assembly was repainted in apparent defiance of the second commandment with a rich assortment of figured scenes in three superimposed tiers above a dado of imitation marble panels, depicting Old Testament episodes such as the sacrifice of Isaac, the Exodus or Moses by the burning bush arranged in no discernible order (Pl. XLVIII). The sophistication of the primarily frontal compositions and the blending of Greek, Mesopotamian, Iranian and Jewish motifs argue the existence then of a complex cycle of Biblical illustrations, otherwise unknown. Lastly, towards A.D. 250 a house room was converted into a Christian baptistry, and again the walls were painted with figured scenes, although somewhat sketchily. The side walls bore Biblical subjects such as David and Goliath, the healing of the paralytic (who appears twice in the same scene, an example of 'continuous narrative'), the walking on the water and perhaps the women at the Sepulchre, while the back wall behind the font contained the main painting of a beardless, short-haired Christ as the Good Shepherd, carrying one sheep and surrounded by others, with Adam and Eve in loin cloths added afterwards to make the doctrinal point that after man's Fall he was to be redeemed through Christ (Pl. XLVIIc). Although some of the repertoire corresponds with that of the Christian catacombs of Rome, the Durene scenes of David and Goliath and the women at the tomb are lacking there, and the loin cloth of Adam and Eve are idiosyncratic.

So the full picture of religious activity in western Asia in the Parthian period is a rich and varied one, as is its illustration in art.

CATALOGUE OF ILLUSTRATIONS

Plate I

Air view of Palmyra, Syria, from the south-east: in the foreground the temple of Bel in its walled sacred area (*haram*), with triumphal arch, market place, colonnaded streets and tombs beyond; on the temple see H. Seyrig, *AS* I, 102-109; *AS* III, 115-124; M. Gawlikowski, *Le temple palmyrénien*, Warsaw 1973, 53ff.; H. J. W. Drijvers, *The religion of Palmyra*, Leiden 1976, 9-13, 23; M. A. R. Colledge, *The art of Palmyra*, London 1976, 26-40, 237-238; R. Amy, H. Seyrig and E. Will (forthcoming); photo InfA 541/22.

Plate II

Plans of 'broad room' temples: (A) Aï Khanum, 'Idented' temple, phase IV, *c*. 300-250 B.C., from P. Bernard, *CRAI*, 1971, 385-452, fig.17; (B) Uruk (Warka), chapel in the Anu-Antum precinct, first or second centuries, A.D., from C. Hopkins, *Berytus* VII, 1942, 1-18, fig.1; (C) Uruk (Warka), temple of Gareus, built before A.D. 110, after C. Hopkins, *Berytus* VII, 1942, 1-18, fig.2; (D) Assur, 'Peripteros' temple, later Parthian period, after C. Hopkins, *Berytus* VII, 1942, 1-18, fig.3; (E) Hatra, shrine VI, second century A.D., from H. J. Lenzen, *AA*, 1955, 356, fig.7; (F) Dura-Europos, temple of Artemis in the third century A.D., from A. Perkins, *The art of Dura-Europos*, Oxford 1973, fig.3; (G) Palmyra, temple of Bel, *c*. A.D. 32, from D. Schlumberger, *L'orient hellénisé*, Paris 1970 fig.29; cf. Colledge, *Parthian art*, 37.

Plate III

a) Temples of 'centralized square' plan: (A) Susa, fourth or third century B.C. (B) Persepolis, 'Fratadara' temple, *c*. 300-250 B.C.; (C) Kuh-i Khwaja, early Parthian period (?); (D) Taxila, Jandial temple, Indo-Scythian period, probably first century B.C.; from K. Schippmann, *Die iranischen Feuerheiligtümer*, Berlin 1971, fig.83; cf. Colledge, *Parthian art*, 43-45.

b) Plan of the sanctuary of the Sun, Hatra, first to third centuries A.D.: (A) Great south *iwan*; (B) Sanctuary of 'Shamash', of 'centralized square' plan; (C) Temple of Shahru; (D) 'Greek' or 'Hellenistic' temple, of Roman plan, perhaps first and second centries A.D.; (E) Cistern; (F) Gate, after W. Andrae, *Hatra*, I, II, *WVDOG* 9, 21, Berlin 1908, 1912, pl. III.

Plate IV

a) Khurha, Iran, two columns from temple precinct colonnade, perhaps second century B.C.; photo E. Herzfeld, *Iran in the ancient east*, Oxford 1941, Pl. LXXXVIII, courtesy Mrs. C. M. Bradford.

b) Old Nisa, Turkmenistan, U.S.S.R., reconstruction of the 'Square Hall' as rebuilt in the mid-Parthian period, with quadrilobate columns and walls divided into two superimposed registers with niches containing clay figures (of ancestors?) photo G. A. Pugachenkova, *VDI,* 1951 (4), 191f., fig.3.

c) Hatra, Iraq, great north and (on left) south limestone *iwans* of Sun sanctuary before restoration, second century A.D. (cf. above, Pl.III, b, A); see W. Andrae, *Hatra*, I, II, *WVDOG*, 9, 21, Berlin 1908, 1912; F. Safar and M. A. Mustafa, *Hatra: city of the Sun God* (in Arabic), Baghdad 1974; photo Dir. Ant., Baghdad.

Plate V

a) Palmyra, Syria, limestone temple of Bel, *c.* A.D. 32 (see above, Pl.I); inscription: Cantineau, *Inventaire des inscriptions de Palmyre*, IX, Beirut 1933, 1; photo D. Schlumberger, *L'orient hellénisé.*

b) Palmyra, Syria, limestone tomb-tower of Elahbel before restoration, completed A.D. 103; see T. Wiegand, *Palmyra*, Berlin 1932, 48, Pl.29; M. Gawlikowski, *Monuments funéraires de Palmyre*, Warsaw 1970, 86-91; M. A. R. Colledge, *The art of Palmyra*, London 1976, 60; inscription: J. Cantineau, *Inventaire des inscriptions de Palmyre*, IV, Beirut 1931, no.27a; *CIS*, II, 4134; photo InfA 315.

c) Palmyra, Syria, reconstruction of the third-century A.D. limestone west recess (*exedra*) within the underground tomb (*hypogeum*) of Iarḥai; Damascus Museum; see H. Seyrig and R. Amy, *Syria* 17, 1936, 229-266; H. Seyrig, *Syria* 27, 1950; *AS*, 46; M. Gawlikowski, *Monuments funéraires de Palmyre*, Warsaw 1970, 111-113; Colledge, *Art of Palmyra*, 60; photo InfA.

Plate VI

a) Nemrud Dağ, Commagene, Turkey, colossal head of Zeus-Oromasdes from *hierothesion* west terrace; *c.* 69-31 B.C. on site; limestons, height *c.* 2 m.; see Humann, *Reisen*; Ghirshman, *Iran*, Pl.73; Waldmann, *Kultref.*, Pl.XVIII.2; Colledge, *Parthian art*, 83; photo K. Rintelen, Münster, courtesy Dr. F. K. Dörner.

b) Nemrud Dağ, Commagene, Turkey, relief of handshake (*dexiosis*) between the seated god Zeus-Oromasdes and king Antiochus I of Commagene; *c.* 69-31 B.C.; on site; limestone, height *c.* 2 m.; see Humann, *Reisen*; drawing Waldmann, *Kultref.*, Pl.XXII.1.

c) Nemrud Dağ, Commagene, Turkey, colossal statues on the east terrace of the *hierothesion* of king Antiochus I of Commagene: (from left to right) Antiochus I, the Tyche of Commagene, Zeus-Oromasdes, Apollo-Mithras-Helios-Hermes and Artagnes-Heracles-Ares: *c.* 69-31 B.C.; on site; limestone, height *c.* 8 m.; sec Humann, *Reisen*; Waldmann, *Kultref.*; Colledge, *Parthian art*, 83, Pl.4; photo K. Rintelen, Münster, courtesy Dr. F. K. Dörner.

Plate VII

a) Nemrud Dağ, Commagene, Turkey, colossal head of Apollo-Mithras-Helios-Hermes from *hierothesion* east terrace; *c.* 69-31 B.C.; on site; limestone, height *c.* 2 m.; see

Humann, *Reisen*; Waldmann, *Kultref.*, Pl.XIX.1; photo K. Rintelen, Münster, courtesy Dr. F. K. Dörner.

b) Nemrud Dağ, Commagene, Turkey, relief of handshake (*dexiosis*) between the god Apollo-Mithras-Helios-Hermes and king Antiochus I of Commagene; *c.* 69-31 B.C.; on site; limestone, height *c.* 2 m.; see Humann, *Reisen*; Ghirshman, *Iran*, Pl.80; Waldmann, *Kultref.*, Pl.XXII.3; photo K. Rintelen, Münster, courtesy Dr. F. K. Dörner.

c) Bard-i Nishandeh, west Iran, column capital from 'temple of Anahita and Mithra' with a relief figure on each face including this standing male god (Mithra?); late Parthian period; Susa Museum, site no. GBN 171C; limestone, height 53; see R. Ghirshman, *Illustrated London News*, July 16, 1966, 18-19, fig.8; R. Ghirshman, *Terrasses sacrées*, *MDAI* 15, Paris 1976, I, 45-46, 192-193, 205, II, Pls.XXIV, 18.C; illustration courtesy Madame T. Ghirshman.

Plate VIII

a) Nemrud Dağ, Commagene, Turkey, colossal head of Artagnes-Heracles-Ares from *hierothesion* west terrace; *c.* 69-31 B.C.; on site; limestone, height *c.* 2 m.; see Humann, *Reisen*; Ghirshman, *Iran,* Pl.76; Waldmann, *Kultref.*, pl.XX.2; photo K. Rintelen, courtesy Dr. F. K. Dörner.

b) Arsameia on the Nymphaios (Eski Kâhta). Commagene, Turkey, relief of handshake (*dexiosis*) between the god Artagnes-Heracles-Ares and king Antiochus I (or possibly his father king Mithradates I Kallinikos) of Commagene; *c.* 69-31 B.C.; on site; limestone, height 2.26 m.; see Ghirshman, *Iran*, Pl.79; J. H. Young, in F. K. Dörner and T. Goell, 'Arsameia', *Istanbuler Forschungen* 23, 1963, 203-208, 223, 226, Pl.27.48-51; J. H. Young, *AJA* 68, 1964, 33-34; Waldmann, *Kultref.*, Pl.XXXI; Colledge, *Parthian art*, 99, Pl.32b; photo K. Rintelen, courtesy Dr. F. K. Dörner.

c) Tang-i Butân, Shîmbâr valley, Elymais, west Iran, rock relief showing four juxtapoed groups of one or more worshippers beside a 'Heracles' (Verethraghna?) figure, added successively from left to right; *c.* A.D. 100-200; height *c.* 2 m.; see A. D. H. Bivar, *BSOAS* 27, 1964, 265-290, Pls.I, II; Colledge, *Parthian art*, 92, Pl.18; photo J. Hansman.

Plate IX

a) Masjid-i Solaiman, west Iran, area of 'temple of Heracles', statue of nude 'Heracles' (Verethraghna?) strangling the Nemean lion; late Parthian period; Susa Museum, site no. GMIS 30; limestone, height 2.40 m.; see R. Ghirshman, *CRAI*, 1968, 11-12, 15, fig.3; R. Ghirshman, *Terrasses sacrées*, *MDAI* 15, 1976, I, 91-94, 119-120, 264-268, II, Pls.LXX, LXXXIX.5, 23-24; illustration courtesy Madame T. Ghirshman.

b) Masjid-i Solaiman, west Iran, antecella of 'temple of Heracles', relief of 'Heracles' (Verethraghna?) reclining (*cubans*), wearing tunic, trousers and shoes, with cup, bow and quiver; mid- to late-Parthian period; Susa Museum, site no. GMIS 20; grey limestone, size 28 × 22; see R. Ghirshman, *CRAI*, 1968, 12, fig.1; R. Ghirshman, *Terrasses sacrées*, MDAI 15, 1976, I, 95, 120, II, Pls.LXXXVI.1, 25; illustration courtesy Madame T. Ghirshman.

Plate X

a) Bard-i Nishandeh, west Iran, column capital from 'temple of Anahita and Mithra' with a relief figure on each face including this standing goddess (Anahita?); late Parthian period: Susa Museum, site no. GBN 171A; limestone, height 53; see R. Ghirshman, *Illustrated London News*, July 16, 1966, 18-19, fig.9; R. Ghirshman, *Terrasses sacrées*, *MDAI* 15, 1976, I, 45-46, 192-193, 205, II, Pls.XXIV, 18.A; illustration courtesy Madame T. Ghirshman.

b) Iran, figurine of nude female (Anahita?); first to third centuries A.D.; Staatliche Museen, Islamische Abteilung, Berlin-Dahlem; bronze, height 11.5; see Colledge, *Parthian art*, 87-88, Pl.11b; photo Staatliche Museen, Islamische Abteilung, Berlin.

c) Tang-i Sarvak, Elymais, west Iran, detail of reliefs on the second isolated rock (II), showing figures and a cult object (baetyl?); *c.* A.D.150-225; in situ; height *c.* 3 m.; see M. A. Stein, *Old routes of western Irân*, London 1940, 104ff., figs.29-37, 42; N. C. Debevoise, *JNES* 1, 1942, 97-102 W. B. Henning, *Asia Major* 2 (2), 1952, 151-78, Pls.i-xx; Colledge, *Parthian art*, 92, Pl.19; photo E. Smekens, courtesy Prof. Dr. L. Vanden Berghe and the Belgian Archaeological Expedition in Iran.

Plate XI

a) Drawings of seal-impressions: (A) to (E) from Hecatompylus (Shahr-i Qumis), north-east Iran, *c.* 50 B.C., courtesy of J. Hansman; (F) to (M) from Old Nisa, Russian Turkestan, the 'Treasury' in the mid-Parthian period, from M. E. Masson and G. A. Pugachenkova, *VDI*, 1954, 163; cf. Colledge, *Parthian art*, 103, fig.42.

b) Tang-i Sarvak, Elymais, west Iran, detail of reliefs on second isolated rock (II), showing male figure wrestling with a lion; *c.* A.D.150-225; in situ; height *c.* 2 m.; see above, Pl.Xc; photo E. Smekens, courtesy Prof. Dr. L. Vanden Berghe and the Belgian Archaeological Expedition in Iran.

Plate XII

a) Nemrud Dağ, Commagene, Turkey, fragmentary relief of an investiture with a 'ring of office' from the *hierothesion* east terrace; *c.* 69-31 B.C.; on site; limestone, height *c.* 1 m.; see Waldmann, *Kultref.*, Pl.XXIV.3; cf. Colledge, *Parthian art*, 99, 129; photo Waldmann, *Kultref.*, Pl.XXXIV.3.

b) Nemrud Dağ, Commagene, Turkey, relief of a lion-horoscope from the *hierothesion*: *c.* 69-31 B.C. (7 July, 62 B.C.?); on site; limestone, height *c.* 1.5 m.; see Humann, *Reisen*, pl.XI; J. H. Young, in F. K. Dörner and T. Goell, 'Arsameia', *Istanbuler Forschungen* 23, 1963, 226-227; Waldmann, *Kultref.*, Pl.XV.2; photo Humann, *Reisen*, Pl.XI.

c) Tang-i Sarvak, Elymais, west Iran, reliefs on the second isolated rock (II), face b, showing (lower register) three standing figures, and (upper register) the investiture of the reclining local king Worôd before three figures, probably deities, most likely (from left to right) the seated Mithra and Anahita, and the standing Ahura Mazda-Bel; *c.* A.D.150-225; in situ; height of rock *c.* 6 m.; see above, Pl.Xc, and H. Seyrig, *Syria* 47,

1970, 113-116, Pl.IX.3; *AS*, 90; R. Ghirshman, *CRAI*, 1974, 40-41, fig.4: photo E. Smekens, courtesy Prof. Dr. L. Vanden Berghe and the Belgian Archaeological Expedition in Iran.

Plate XIII

a) Bard-i Nishandeh, west Iran, north staircase, relief of a king casting incense on a burner before four male figures (priests and attendants ?); *c.* A.D. 200-225; Teheran Museum 4287, site no. GBN 30; limestone, size 55 × 107 × 39; see R. Ghirshman, *Syria* 41, 1964, 307-308, Pl.XX.1; R. Ghirshman, *Illustrated London News*, July 4, 1964, 14, fig.2; R. Ghirshman, *CRAI*, 1975, fig.4; R. Ghirshman, *Terrasses sacrées*, *MDAI* 15, 1976, I, 21 23, 26, 271, II, Pl.XIII.3; cf. Colledge, *Parthian art*, 99, Pl.31b; photo Muzeh-e Iran-e Bastan, Teheran, courtesy Madame T. Chirshman.

b) Bisutun (Behistun), west Iran, adjacent rock reliefs showing (left) a Parthian monarch (Mithradates II?) before four dignitaries (*c.* 123-110 B.C.?), and (right) Gotarzes I or II 'Geopothros' defeating an adversary in a combat on horseback, *c.* 100-80 B.C. or *c.* A.D.50; total height of relief field *c.* 4 m.; see E. Herzfeld, *Am Tor von Asien*, Berlin 1920, 36-41, 46-47, fig.12, Pls.XXI - XXIII; E. Herzfeld, *Archaeological History of Iran*, Oxford 1935, 54-57; N. C. Debevoise, *JNES* 1, 1942, 96-97; Ghirshman, *Iran*, 56, 126, 264, fig.64; M. A. R. Colledge, *The Parthians*, London 1967, fig.4; D. Schlumberger, *L'orient hellénisé*, Paris 1970, 40, 152; W. Kleiss, *AMI* n.f.3, 1970, 133, Pl.67; Colledge, *Parthian art*, 90-91, Pl.15: photo E. Herzfeld, *Am Tor von Asien*, Pl.XXI, courtesy Mrs. C. M. Bradford.

c) Tang-i Sarvak, Elymais, west Iran, reliefs on the second isolated rock (II), face a, showing (lowest register) male figure wrestling with a lion (see above, Pl.XIb), (central register) six frontal males and a horseman, and (top register) perhaps a king and queen enthroned, with attendants, and a standing figure and cult item (baetyl? see Pl.Xc); see above, Pl.Xc; photo E. Smekens, courtesy Prof. Dr. L. Vanden Berghe and the Belgian Archaeological Expedition in Iran.

Plate XIV

a) Khaltchayan, north Bactria, central Asia, wall reliefs from the 'reception hall', showing (A) the central group of a royal couple with high-ranking persons, and (B) the north part of the main wall with a seated noble, high-ranking clansmen and a goddess on a chariot; (C) south wall, mounted archers; probably *c.* 50 B.C. - A.D.50; painted clay, height *c.* 1.80 m.; see G. A. Pugachenkova, *Skulptura Khaltchayana*, Moscow 1971; cf. Colledge, *Parthian art*, fig.40; drawings Pugachenkova, *Skulptura*, 51, 61.

b) Kuh-i Khwaja, east Iran, wall painting of a king and queen once in the north 'gallery' of the building complex; first to third centuries A.D.; metallic oxide paints on smoothed plaster; see E. Herzfeld, *Archaeological history of Iran*, Oxford 1935, 66-75, Pl.CIV; Ghirshman, *Iran*, 45, Pl.56; G. Gullini, *Architettura iranica*, Turin 1964, 443-453; D. Schlumberger, *L'Orient hellénisé*, Paris 1970, 54; Colledge, *Parthian art*, 119; photo Herzfeld, *Archaeological history*, Pl.CIV, courtesy Mrs. C. M. Bradford.

Plate XV

a) Nemrud Dağ, Commagene, Turkey, relief of royal ancestor Xerxes I on the west terrace of the *hierothesion* of king Antiochus I of Commagene; *c.* 69-31 B.C.; on site; limestone, height *c.* 2 m.; see Humann, *Reisen*; Waldmann, *Kultref.*, Pl.XXIII.3; photo Waldmann.

b) Shami, west Iran, statue of chieftain in Iranian dress and hairstyle from the shrine; *c.* 50 B.C.-A.D.150; Teheran Museum 2401; hollow-cast bronze, height 1.90 m.; see especially H. Seyrig, *Syria* 20, 1939, 177-183, Pl.XXV; A. Godard, *The art of Iran*, London 1965, 156-158, Pls.94-95; D. Schlumberger, *L'Orient hellénisé*, Paris 1970, 156, 157, 160, Pl.23; Colledge, *Parthian art*, 86, Pl.12; photo Anvar, Teheran.

c) Surkh Kotal, Afghanistan, Kushan sanctuary, statue of a Kushan prince; *c.* A.D.130; Kabul Museum, Afghanistan; limestone, height *c.* 1.20 m.; see C. M. Kieffer, *Marg* 15, March 1962 (2), 46-47, figs.3, 5; Ghirshman, *Iran*, 274, Pl.361; D. Schlumberger, *L'orient hellénisé*, Paris 1970, 64-65, fig. 28; Colledge, *Parthian art*, 87, Pl.14a; photo DAFA.

d) Mathura, north India, Mât shrine, Kushan dynastic statue of the deceased king Vima Kadphises; *c.* A.D.130; Mathura Museum (Muttra, Curzon Museum) no.215; sandstone, height 2.08 m.; see B. Rowland, *Art and architecture of India*, London 1952, 85-86, Pl.43; C. M. Kieffer, *Marg* 15, March 1962 (2), 46-47, fig.11; J. M. Rosenfield, *Dynastic arts of the Kushans*, California 1967, 144-145, fig. 1; Colledge, *Parthian art*, 87; photo Government Museum, Mathura (Muttra), negative 73.211.

Plate XVI

Persian, Seleucid and Parthian coins (double letters indicate reverses):

a) Gold daric of 'Darius I' in kneeling-running attitude, early fifth century B.C.;
b) Silver drachm struck at Iasus (?) with a Persian satrap's head, *c.* 395 B.C.(?);
c) Silver tetradrachm of Seleucus I with head of Heracles and (cc) seated Zeus, 312-281 B.C.;
d) Silver drachm with diademed head of Ariarathes VI of Cappadocia, C. 123-111 B.C.;
e) Silver drachm of (Autophradates?) king of Persis with his head in a Persian hat and (ee) a figure worshipping at a fire temple, *c.* 250-150 B.C.;
f) Silver drachm with head of king Artaxerxes II of Persis in a turret crown, first century B.C.;
g) Hemidrachm with head of king Manučithr of Persis, second century A.D.;
h) Silver drachm of Mithradates I of Parthia with a 'beardless head' in a bashliq and (hh) a seated 'bowman', *c.* 171-138 B.C.;
i) Silver drachm with bearded head of Mithradates I of Parthia, *c.* 171-138 B.C.;
j) Silver tetradrachm with bearded head of Mithradates I of Parthia and (jj) a standing Heracles, minted at Seleucia and dated 140/39 B.C.;
k) Silver drachm of Mithradates II of Parthia, later type, with his head in the new high tiara and (kk) 'Arsaces' seated on a throne, towards 100 B.C.;

l)   Silver drachm with frontal diademed head of an unknown Parthian king (Mithradates III, or Darius of Media Atropatene?), 57-55 or *c*. 65 B.C.;

mm)   Bronze coin of Orodes II of Parthia with a towered building, *c*. 57-38 B.C.;

n)   Silver drachm with diademed bust of Phraataces of Parthia *c*. 38/7-2 B.C.;

o)   Silver drachm with diademed bust of Phraataces of Parthia and (oo) the diademed bust of queen Musa, A.D. 2-4;

pp)   Silver drachm of Vonones I of Parthia with a diademed Victory carrying a palm branch and a Greek legend commemorating his defeat of Artabanus III, A.D. 8-12;

q)   Silver tetradrachm with frontal head of Artabanus III of Parthia and (qq) Artabanus on horseback receiving the submission of a personified city (Seleucia?), dated A.D. 26-7;

rr)   Bronze coin of Gotarzes II of Parthia with the bust of a queen (his wife?), *c*. A.D. 38-51;

ss)   Bronze coin of Gotarzes II of Parthia with a hand holding a caduceus, *c*. A.D. 38-51;

t)   Silver drachm with the diademed bust of Vologases I of Parthia and, behind his head, the Aramaic letters WL, *c*. A.D. 51-77;

u)   Silver drachm with frontal head of Vardanes II of Parthia, *c*. A.D. 56-8;

vv)   Silver tetradrachm with Pacorus II of Parthia on horseback receiving the submission of a city Tyche and a male subject, dated A.D. 82/3;

w) ww) Silver tetradrachm of Vologases IV (III) of Parthia, dated A.D. 164/5;

x)   Silver drachm with frontal head of Vologases V (IV) of Parthia, A.D. 190/1-206/7;

yy)   Silver drachm of Artavasdes of Parthia with seated 'Arsaces', Aramaic letters ('RT) WZY' NLK, and blundered Greek text, *c*. A.D. 226-7(?); British Museum; actual size; cf. Colledge, *Parthian art*, 103-106, Pl.38; photo Gardner.

Plate XVII

Coins of Parthian subjects, and of Bactrian and Indian rulers (double letters indicate reverses):

a)   Silver tetradrachm with jugate busts of Kamnaskires II and queen Anzaze of Elymais, dated 82/1 B.C.;

b)   Silver tetradrachm with frontal head of Kamnaskires Orodes of Elymais, late first century A.D.;

c)   Silver tetradrachm of Tiraios II of Characene, 78/7-48/7 B.C.;

d)   Bronze tetradrachm with head of Magha of Characene in diadem and tiara, *c*. A.D. 195-210;

e)   Bronze coin of Antiochus I of Commagene with a beardless head in Armenian tiara and (ee) a lion, *c*. 69-31 B.C.;

ff)   Bronze coin of Septimius Severus and Abgar VIII of Osrhoene (minted at Edessa) with the head of Abgar in diadem and tiara, *c*. A.D. 200;

gg)   Bronze municipal coin of Nineveh with a galloping horse, *c*. 124/3-90 B.C.;

h)   Attic-standard gold stater of Diodotus I or II of Bactria, with a diademed head of Diodotus and (hh) a naked Zeus, thundering, later third century B.C.;

i)   Attic-standard silver tetradrachm with the head of Demetrius I of Bactria in an elephant-scalp cap, *c.* 200-185 B.C.;

j)   Rectangular bronze punch-marked coin from Taxila, fourth to second century B.C.;

k)   Attic-standard silver hemidrachm of Apollodotus I of India with an elephant and Greek legend and (kk) a humped bull and Kharosthi text, *c.* 170 B.C.(?);

l)   Indian-standard square silver drachm of Apollodotus I of India with an elephant and Greek legend and (ll) a humped bull and Kharosthi text, *c.* 170 B.C.(?);

m)   Indian-standard round silver drachm of Menander ('Soter') of India, with his diademed and helmeted bust and (mm) a 'spear-thrusting' Athena, Pushkalâvatî monogram, *c.* 155-146 B.C.(?);

n)   Square bronze coin of Menander ('Soter') of India with diademed 'spear-thruster' bust, *c.* 155-146 B.C.(?);

o)   Indian-standard round silver tetradrachm with jugate busts of Strato and Agathocleia of India, later second century B.C.;

p)   Indian-standard round silver drachm of Hermaeus of India, *c.* 120 B.C.;

q)   Barbarous Indian-standard round bronze coin of 'Hermaeus', later first century B.C.(?);

r)   Silver tetradrachm of Maues of India, with standing Zeus, *c.* 85-77 B.C.(?);

s)   Silver tetradrachm of Azes I of India with a horseman and (ss) Zeus standing, 57 B.C. or soon after;

t)   Silver tetradrachm with the moustached, diademed head of Heraos (Miaos?) and (tt) a horseman and Greek legend, later first century B.C.(?);

u)   Bronze coin with the moustached, diademed head of the 'Kshatrapa' Râjûvula with (uu) a 'spear-thruster' Athena, *c.* 50-10 B.C.(?);

v)   Bronze coin of the Kushan king Kujula Kadphises with a head of 'Augustus' and Greek legend, earlier to mid first century A.D.(?);

w)   Gold dinar of the Kushan king Vima Kadphises with chariot ('biga'), *c.* A.D. 100(?);

x)   Gold dinar of the Kushan king Kanishka I with the king sacrificing by a fire altar and (xx) the Buddha, frontal, and 'Bactrian' legend BODDO, *c.* A.D. 128-51;

yy)   Silver drachm of king Shapur of Persis, with head (of his father Papak?) and Aramaic legend, *c.* A.D. 210-5(?); British Museum; actual size; cf. Colledge, *Parthian art*, 106-109, Pl.39; photo Gardner.

Plate XVIII

a) Hung-i Nauruzi, Elymais, west Iran, rock relief with a profile mounted king and attendant (left), and four frontal males; perhaps *c.* 50 B.C. - A.D. 50; in situ; height *c.* 4 m.; see L. Vanden Berghe, *Iranica Antiqua* 3, 1963, 155-168, Pls. 53-55; D. Schlumberger, *L'orient hellénisé*, Paris 1970, 40, 152, Pl.6; R. Ghirshman, *CRAI*, 1975, 56, fig.3; Colledge, *Parthian art*, 92, Pl.17; photo E. Smekens, courtesy Prof. Dr. L. Vanden Berghe and the Belgian Archaeological Expedition in Iran.

b) Bisutun (Behistun), west Iran, rock relief of a Parthian ruler (Mithradates II?) before four dignitaries, as sketched by Grelot in 1673-4 before eighteenth-century damage; *c.* 123-110 B.C.(?); in situ; height *c.* 4 m.; see above, Pl.XIIIb; from E. Herzfeld, *Am Tor von Asien*, Berlin 1920, fig.11.

c) Susa, west Iran, inscribed (funerary?) relief depicting the Parthian king Artabanus V handing the ring of office to Khwasak, satrap of Susa; dated 14 September, A.D.215; Teheran Museum 2844; limestone, height 89.5; see especially R. Ghirshman, *Monuments Piot* 44, 1950, 97-107, Pl.XI; W. B. Henning, Asia Major 2, 1952, 176; D. Schlumberger, *L'orient hellénisé*, Paris 1970, 155, Pl.25; Colledge, *Parthian art*, 98, Pl.29; photo Muzeh-e Iran-e Bastan, Teheran.

Plate XIX

Palmyra, Syria, religious tokens (tesserae; numbers refer to the following publication): (a) 119: nude Apollo figure with name 'Nebû' (top left), with bust of god (Bel?), Victory and (as seal impressions) head of Apollo, and Hermes (b) 390: long- (horse?) eared frontal head or mask; (c) 118: aedicula with triad of Bel (?), cuirassed; (d) 83: globules, with 'Listen, Bel. The Benê Bolaᶜa'; (e) 182: bust of helmeted god between two baetyls (?); (f) 435: seated priest with crater and ladle; (g) 945: vase, leaves and rosettes; (h) 934: seal imprint, with Tyche; (i) 168 face a: Apollo and Heracles figures standing; (j) 168 face b: nude Dionysus figure standing, with palm, cornucopia and cantharus; (k) 174 face a: standing frontal cuirassed god in sleeved tunic, trousers and bell-shaped helmet (Arṣû ?); (l) 19: priest on couch under vine with servant, and (gem imprint) Hermes; (m) 174 face b: dromedary, and nude Hermes figure; (n) 725: two servants, branches, crater, two acanthus leaves and (gem imprint) Apollo; (o) 422: two cloaked figures sacrificing on a burner; (p) 139: bust of radiate, cuirassed god, probably Shamash (apparently named on the reverse); (q) 396: profile bust with crescent; (r) 660: grapes between vine leaves; (s) 724: two standing priests casting incense on a burner, stars, palms and (gem imprint) bust of Athena; (t) 285 face b: two standing gods in short tunic with round shield and lance, probably Maᶜanû and Shaᶜarû; (v) 285 face a: female figure, and (right) standing Artemis figure named NNY, 'Nanai'; (w) 313: (gem imprint) winged Nemesis in calathos with wheel, and radiate bust; (x) 166: female bust, named beneath ʾNHYT, 'Anahit(a)'; (y) 28: triad of Bel (who is named on the reverse), Iarḥibôl (to our left) and ᶜAglibôl (right); (z) 792: bust of priest; (aa) 254: busts of two similar beardless gods (Maᶜanû and Shaᶜarû ?); (bb) 302: standing Apollo figure with lyre in sleeved tunic, with name 'Nebû'; first to third centuries A.D.; British Museum; terracotta, roughly actual size; see H. Ingholt, H. Seyrig and J. Starcky, *Recueil des tessères de Palmyre*, Paris 1955; C. Dunant, *Syria* 36, 1959, 102-110; M. A. R. Colledge, *The Art of Palmyra*, London 1976, 54-56, Pl.54; photo British Museum, courtesy of the Trustees.

Plate XX

a) Al Maqateᶜ, near Palmyra, Syria, relief with five labelled deities, (from left) Malakbel - Baᶜalshamîn - Bel - ᶜAglibôl - Astarte; *c.* A.D.100-150; Palmyra Museum

2195B; limestone, size 52 × 93 × 21; see A. Bounni, in *Mélanges K. Michalowski*, Warsaw 1966, 313-314, fig.2; A. Bounni, *AAS* 17, 1967 (2), 25ff.; H. Seyrig, *Syria* 48, 1971, 97, 113, fig.4; Drijvers, *Religion*, 11-12, 24, Pl.X.1 Colledge, *Palmyra*, 46.

b) Palmyra, Syria, (architectural ?) relief with four unnamed gods, probably (from left) Iarḥibôl - Bel - ʿAglibôl - Arṣû (?); first or second century A.D.; Palmyra Museum; limestone, size 95 × 105; see especially H. Seyrig, *Syria* 13, 1932, 190-195, Pl.XLII = *AS* 6; H. Seyrig, *Syria* 48, 1971, 111 = *AS* 93; Drijvers, *Religion*, 11, 24, Pl.VII; Colledge, *Palmyra*, 46; photo InfA F547.

c) Jabal al Merah, near Palmyra, Syria, relief with a worshipper casting incense before four named gods, (from left) Arṣû - Iarḥibôl - Bel - ʿAglibôl; *c.* A.D.100, Palmyra Museum 1233A; limestone, size 47 × 55 × 15; see A. Bounni, in *Mélanges K. Michalowski*, Warsaw 1966, 317-318, fig.3; A. Bounni, *AAS* 17, 1967 (2), 25ff.; H. Seyrig, *Syria* 48, 1971, 90, 111, fig.1 = *AS* 93; Drijvers, *Religion*, 11, 24, Pl.IX.1; Colledge, *Palmyra*, 51; photo InfA F4200.

Plate XXI

a) Wadi ʿArafa, near Palmyra, Syria, relief with a worshipper (on our left) casting incense before seven (originally eight) named deities, (from left) Astarte - ʿAglibôl -Malakbel - Bel - Baʿalshamîn - Nemesiṣ - Arṣû (and Abgal); dated November, A.D.152; Palmyra Museum 1234A; limestone, size 28 × 58 × 17; see A. Bounni, in *Mélanges K. Michalowski*, Warsaw 1966, 317-318, fig.4; A. Bounni, *AAS* 17, 1967 (2), 25ff.; H. Seyrig, *Syria* 48, 1971, 97, 101, 112, 113, fig.3; Drijvers, *Religion*, 12, 24, Pl.X.2; Colledge, *Palmyra*, 51; photo InfA F4210.

b) Palmyra, Syria, fragmentary relief with four (originally six) deities standing (from left) goddess - Iarḥibôl (?) - Bel (?) - ʿAglibôl (named above), and bust of solar god in pediment; dated January, A.D.119 (?); National Museum, Damascus; limestone, size 53 × 54 × 8; see especially H. Seyrig, *Syria* 13, 1932, 191-192, fig.3 = *AS* I, 28, fig.3; Schlumberger, *Palmyrène*, 91 no.1, Pl.XLI.3; T. Borkowska, *Studia Palmyreńskie* 1, 1966, 116, no. 34; T. Borkowska, in *Mélanges K. Michalowski*, Warsaw 1966, 307-309, fig.1; Drijvers, *Religion*, 11, 24, Pl.VIII.2; Colledge, *Palmyra*, 46, fig.28; photo National Museum of Damascus.

Plate XXII

Dura Europos, east Syria, wall-painting once in a side chapel of the temple of Bel (or 'of the Palmyrene Gods') depicting the eunuch Otes and others casting incense before five unnamed standing deities, including ʿAglibôl (with crescent, left of centre) and perhaps Bel; later second or (more likely) earlier third century A.D.; powdered metallic oxide colours on smoothed plaster, size 105 × 350; see F. Cumont, *Fouilles de Doura-Europos*, Paris 1926, 122-134, Pl.LV; A. Perkins, *The art of Dura-Europos*, Oxford 1973, 45-47, Pl.13; Drijvers *Religion*, Pl.XVIII; photo Cumont, *Fouilles*, Pl.LV.

Plate XXIII

Dura-Europos, east Syria, wall-painting on the north wall of the *pronaos* of the temple of Bel (or 'of the Palmyrene Gods') depicting the sacrifice of the Roman army tribune Julius Terentius to three unnamed militarized gods and (below, left) the named personified Fortunes of Dura-Europos (to our right) and Palmyra; A.D.239; Yale University Art Gallery; powdered metallic oxide colours on smoothed plaster, size 88 × 150; see F. Cumont, *Fouilles de Doura-Europos*, Paris 1926, 89ff., Pls.XLIX-LI; H. Seyrig, *Syria* 13, 1932, 31ff. Pl.XLIII = *AS* I, 31ff.; A. Perkins, *The art of Dura-Europos*, Oxford 1973, 42-45, Pl.12; Drijvers, *Religion*, Pl.XIX; photo Cumont, *Fouilles*, Pl.L.

Plate XXIV

a) Dura-Europos, east Syria, inscribed relief from the temple of Zeus Kyrios depicting a seated god named Zeus Kyrios (in Greek) and Ba°alshamîn (in Aramaic) and a ram-carrying dedicant; dated December, A.D.31; Yale University Art Gallery 1935.45; limestone, size 52 × 35 × 9; see C. Hopkins, *Dura Prelim.*, VII-VIII, New Haven 1939, 292-302, 307-309, Pl.XXXVII; R. Du Mesnil, *Inventaire des inscriptions*, Paris 1939, no.23; P. Collart, *Le sanctuaire de Baalshamin à Palmyre*, I, II, Rome 1969, 202, 210, Pl.CIII.2; A. Perkins, *The art of Dura-Europos*, Oxford 1973, 76-77, Pl.30; Drijvers, *Religion*, Pl.XXV; Colledge, *Parthian art*, 99; S. B. Downey, *Dura Final Rep.*, III, 1, 2, Los Angeles 1977, 31-34, no.10, Pl.IV.10; photo Yale University Art Gallery.

b) Palmyra (?), Syria, relief of three unnamed militarized gods, with °Aglibôl (with crescent) on left, and possibly Ba°alshamîn (centre) and Malakbel; (mid- ?) first century A.D.; Louvre Museum A.O.19801; limestone, size 56 × 69; see especially H. Seyrig, *Syria* 26, 1949, 29-41, Pl.II = *AS* IV, 31-43; M. Morehart, *Berytus* 12, 1956-7, 60-61 no. 13, fig.11; T. Borkowska, *Studia Palmyreńskie* 1, 1966, 116-117 no. 35, fig.12; J. Wais, *Studia Palmyreńskie* 4, 1970, 40-41, fig.34; H. Seyrig, *Syria* 47, 1970, 109, fig.29 = *AS* 89; H. Seyrig, *Syria* 48, 1971, 95, fig.2 = *AS* 93; Drijvers, *Religion*, 16, Pl.XXXIV; Colledge, *Palmyra*, 44, Pl.35; photo Service de Documentation, Louvre, Paris.

c) Dura-Europos, east Syria, naos 3 of the temple of the Gaddé, statuette of Nebû (named) with lyre; *c.* A.D.50-250; Yale University Art Gallery 1938.5304; gypsum, size 24.5 × 18 × 13.5; F. Brown, *Dura Prelim. Rep.*, New Haven 1939, 266, 281, Pl.XXXVI.1; R. Du Mesnil, *Inventaire des inscriptions*, Paris 1939, no. 34; A. Perkins, *The art of Dura-Europos*, Oxford 1973, 110, Pl.49; Drijvers, *Religion* Pl.XXXIV; S. B. Downey, *Dura Final Rep.*, III, 1, 2, Los Angeles 1977, 64-65, no.48, Pl.XII.48; photo Yale University Art Gallery.

Plate XXV

a) Palmyra, Syria, relief of four unnamed deities, (from left) 'Heracles' figure (Nergal ?) - goddess - °Aglibôl - Malakbel (?); first century A.D. (?); National Museum, Damascus, 10050; soft limestone, size 22.5 × 35; see especially H. Seyrig, *Syria* 24, 1944-5, 62, Pl.I = *AS* IV, 1ff.; M. Morehart, *Berytus* 12, 1956-7, 59 no.12, fig.10; H. Seyrig, *Syria* 47, 1970, 107-108, fig.28; Drijvers, *Religion*, 12, Pl.XIV; Colledge, *Palmyra*, 45-46, Pl.36; photo InfA 1764.

b) Hatra, Iraq, shrine V, statuette of 'Heracles' figure; *c.* A.D.100-241; Iraq Museum, Baghdad, IM 56768; Mosul marble, height 60; see N. Al-Asil, *Illustrated London News*, December 25, 1954, 1160, fig.3; H. J. Lenzen, *AA*, 1955, 339, fig.1; D. Homès-Fredericq, *Hatra et ses sculptures parthes*, Istanbul 1963, 50, no.1, Pl.I.1; Al-Salihi, *Sculptures*, 92-93 no.28, fig.43; Safar, *Hatra*, 232, Pl.228; photo Dir. Ant., Baghdad.

c) Hatra, Iraq, shrine VIII, statuette of radiate sun god; *c.* A.D.100-241; Iraq Museum Baghdad, IM 57795; alabaster, 20.3 × 6.3; see S. B. Downey, *AJA* 72, 1968, 211-212; Al-Salihi, *Sculptures*, 31-32, figs. 3-4; Safar, *Hatra*, 274, 282, Pl.268; photo Dir.Ant., Baghdad.

Plate XXVI

a) Hatra, Iraq, sanctuary of the Sun, building A, named relief bust of god Marên; second century A.D.; Hatra, Ht.446; limestone, 120 × 75; see Al-Salihi, *Sculptures*, 123-124 no.50, fig.7; Safar, *Hatra*, 113, Pl.88; photo Dir. Ant., Baghdad.

b) Hatra, Iraq, shrine I, relief bust of solar god: *c.* A.D.100-241; Hatra, Ht.36 (= Mosul Museum, 6); limestone, height 75; see N. Al-Asil, *Illustrated London News*, November 17, 1951, 807, fig.8; H. Ingholt, *Parthian sculptures from Hatra*, New Haven 1954, 24, 43, Pl.VII.1; *Catalogue of the Mosul Museum*, Baghdad 1958, 14-15, fig.2; S. B. Downey, *AJA* 72, 1968, 212, 216; Al-Salihi, *Sculptures*, 27-29, 127-128 no.53, fig.78; Safar, *Hatra*, 176-179, Pls.171-2; photo Dir. Ant., Baghdad.

Plate XXVII

a) Palmyra, Syria, named relief of the cuirassed god Shadrafa; dated March, A.D.55; British Museum, London, 125206; limestone, size 47 × 32; see espcially J. B. Chabot, *Choix d'inscriptions de Palmyre*, Paris 1922, 66, Pl.XXIII.1; H. Ingholt, *Studier over Palmyrensk Skulptur*, Copenhagen 1928, 19 no. PS 1, Pl.I; H. Seyrig, *Berytus* 3, 1936, 137-140, Pl.XXX; M. Morehart, *Berytus* 12, 1956-7, 63 no.17, fig.15; T. Borkowska, *Studia Palmyreńskie* 1, 1966, 118 no. 39, fig.15; Drijvers, *Religion*, 18, Pl.XLVIII; Colledge, *Palmyra*, 42, Pl.27; photo British Museum, courtesy Trustees.

b) Dura-Europos, east Syria, *naos* of temple of Aphlad, inscribed relief of a worshipper casting incense before the standing cuirassed god 'Aphlad, called god of the (Euphrates) village of Anath'; *c.* A.D.54; National Museum, Damascus, 4488; limestone, size 51.5 × 31 × 14; see C. Hopkins, *Dura Prelim. Rep.*, V, 106-112, Pl.XIII; M. I. Rostovtzeff, *Yale Classical Studies* 5, 1935, 226-232, fig.36; A. Perkins, *The art of Dura-Europos*, Oxford 1973, 77-79, Pl.31; Colledge, *Parthian art*, 99, Pl.33; S. B. Downey, *Dura Final Rep.*, III, 1, 2, Los Angeles 1977, 7-9 no.1, Pl.I.1; photo Dura-Europos Publications, Yale University.

c) Palmyra, Syria, two-tiered relief with (upper register) bust of god (Malakbel ?) in civil dress holding thyrsus between griffins, and (lower register) bust of cuirassed god (Malakbel ?) with eagle; first century A.D.; Louvre Museum A.O.19799; limestone, height 33; see especially H. Seyrig, *Syria* 22, 1941, 39-44, Pl.II = *AS* 34; P. Collart, *Le sanctuaire de Baalshamin à Palmyre*, I, II, Rome 1969, 160-161, Pl.XCIX, 2; J. Wais, *Studia Palmyreńskie* 4, 1970, 7-9, fig.1; Drijvers, *Religion*, 13, Pl.XXIV.2; Colledge, *Palmyra*, 33, Pl.14; photo Service de Documentation, Louvre, Paris.

Plate XXVIII

a) Dura-Europos, east Syria, inscribed relief depicting the gods Asherû and Sa'ad *c.*
A.D.50-250; National Museum, Damascus, 10948; gypsum, size 44 × 41 × 8; see C.
Hopkins, *Dura Prelim. Rep.*, VI, 228-240, Pl.XXX.1, 2; R. Du Mesnil, *Inventaire des in-
scriptions*, Paris 1939, no.20; A. Perkins, *The art of Dura-Europos*, Oxford 1973, 96-98,
Pl.39; S. B. Downey, *Dura Final Rep.*, III, 1, 2, Los Angeles 1977, 57-60 no.45,
Pl.XII.45; photo Dura-Europos Publications, Yale University.

b) Khirbet Semrine, north-west of Palmyra, Syria, relief showing a worshipper between
the two named horse-riding gods Abgal and Ashar, with rosettes (stars ?) and a snake (sun
symbol ?); dated October, A.D.154; National Museum, Damascus, C.2842; limestone,
size 57/62 × 50 × 7/10; see especially Schlumberger, *Palmyrène*, 56 no.18, 146 no.6,
Pl.XXII.1; D. Schlumberger, *Syria* 37, 1960, 300, Pl.XI.2; T. Borkowska, *Studia
Palmyreńskie* 1, 1966, 107 no.7; J. T. Milik, *Dédicaces faites par des dieux*, Paris, 1972, 343;
Drijvers, *Religion*, 21, Pl.LXIII.2; Colledge, *Palmyra*, 49-50, Pl.43; photo InfA F2721.

c) Khirbet Abu Duhur, north-west of Palmyra, Syria, relief dedicated to *mlk'* (the god
Malkâ, or 'the kings' ?), showing three gods before two worshippers (on left); dated
February, A.D. 263; National Museum, Damascus, C.2841; limestone, size 53 × 102 ×
16/19; see especially Schlumberger, *Palmyrène*, 02 no 9, 165 no. 57, Pl.XXXVIII.2; T.
Borkowska, *Studia Palmyreńskie* 1, 1966, 112 no.23; J. Wais, *Studia Palmyreńskie* 4, 1970, 39,
fig.32; Drijvers, *Religion*, 18, Pl.XLVI.1; Colledge, *Palmyra*, 50-51, Pl.42; photo InfA
920.

Plate XXIX

a) Dura-Europos, east Syria, *naos* 3 of temple of the Gaddé, inscribed relief of the Fortune (Gad) of Dura-Europos; dated April, A.D.159; Yale University Art Gallery
1938.5314; limestone, size 45 × 62 × 13/16.5; see F. Brown, *Dura Prelim. Rep.*, VII-VIII,
New Haven 1939, 258-260, 277-278, Pl.XXXIII; R. Du Mesnil, *Inventaire des inscriptions*,
Paris 1939, 16f., nos.28-30; A. Perkins, *The art of Dura-Europos*, Oxford 1973, 82-84,
Pl.33; S. B. Downey, *Dura Final Rep.* III, 1, 2, Los Angeles 1977, 14-17 no.4, Pl.III.4;
photo Dura-Europos Publications, Yale University.

b) Dura-Europos, east Syria, *naos* 3 of temple of the Gaddé, inscribed relief of the Fortune (Gad) of Palmyra; dated April, A.D.159; Yale University Art Gallery 1938.5313;
limestone, size 47 × 57; see F. Brown, *Dura Prelim. Rep.*, VII-VIII, New Haven 1939,
260-262, 275, 278, Pl.XXXIV; R. Du Mesnil, *Inventaire des inscriptions*, Paris 1939, 17,
nos. 31-32; A. Perkins, *The art of Dura-Europos*, Oxford 1973, 79-82, Pl.32; S. B. Downey,
Dura Final Rep., III, 1, 2, Los Angeles 1977, 17-19 no. 5, Pl.III.5; photo Dura-Europos
Publications, Yale University.

Plate XXX

a) Hatra, Iraq, sanctuary of the Sun, building A, named relief bust of god Bar-Marên;
second century A.D.; Hatra, Ht.443; limestone, 120 × 75; see Al-Salihi, *Sculptures*, 126
no. 52, fig.77; F. Safar, *Sumer* 27, 1971, Pl.8; Safar, *Hatra*, 114-115, Pl.90; photo Dir.
Ant., Baghdad.

b) Hatra, Iraq, in front of Sun sanctuary great north iwan, mask of Dionysus inscribed 'Sha𝑐dû [made it] for Bar-Marên'; *c.* A.D.100-241; Iraq Museum, Baghdad, IM 73014 (= Ht.347); bronze, size 23.7 × 23.6; see Al-Salihi, *Sculptures*, 146-147 no. 63, fig.89; *Safar, Hatra*, 157, Pl.147, 413, inscription 222; photo Dir. Ant., Baghdad.

c) Hatra, Iraq, shrine V, statue of god identified as Aššur-Bel or (more likely) Apollo of Hierapolis; *c.* A.D.100-241; Iraq Museum, Baghdad, IM 56766; Mosul marble, height 112; see especially N. Al-Asil, *Illustrated London News* 6035, 18 December, 1954, 1116, figs.5-6; H. J. Lenzen, *AA*, 1955, 345, figs.2-3; J. Pirenne, *Sacra Pagina* 1, 1959, 297; J. B. Ward Perkins, in *Atti del convegno sul tema; La Persia e il mondo greco-romano*, Rome (Accademia Lincei) 1966, 406; D. Schlumberger, *L'orient hellénisé*, Paris 1970, 143-144, Pl.19a, b; H. Seyrig, *Syria* 49, 1972, 107-108, fig.7; Safar, *Hatra*, 236-241, Pl.227; Colledge, *Parthian art*, 84, Pl.10a; photo Dir. Ant., Baghdad.

Plate XXXI

a) Hatra, Iraq, from back wall of room 13 in Shrine I, relief of an unnamed standing frontal god (Hadad ?) and seated goddess (Atargatis ?) with religious standards, axe, lions, three-headed dog, eagles, snakes, scorpions and bells, painted in black and red; *c.* A.D.100-241; Ht.34 (= Mosul Museum, 11); greenish-grey marble, size 90 × 75 × 16; see especially N. Al-Asil, *Illustrated London News*, 17 November, 1951, 807, fig.11; H. Ingholt, *Parthian sculptures from Hatra*, New Haven 1954, 32-35, Pl.VII.2; S. Fukai, *East and West* 11, 1960, 156-159, Pl.18; S. B. Downey, *AJA* 72, 1968, 214; Al-Salihi, *Sculptures*, 29, 55-60, figs. 19-20; D. Schlumberger, *L'orient hellénisé*, Paris 1970, 140; J. T. Milik, *Dédicaces faites par des dieux*, Paris 1972, 165-166; Safar, *Hatra*, 190, Pl.183; Colledge, *Parthian art*, 100, Pl.35; photo Dir. Ant., Baghdad.

b) Dura-Europos, east Syria, court of temple of Atargatis, relief of an unnamed goddess (Atargatis ?) and god (Hadad ?) enthroned flanking a religious standard, with lions and bulls; *c.* A.D.50-250; Yale University Art Gallery 1938.5343; gypsum (with paint traces), size 41 × 28 × 11.5; see C. Baur, *Dura Prelim. Rep.*, III, New Haven 1933, 100-139, Pl.XIV; A. Perkins, *The art of Dura-Europos*, Oxford 1973, 94-96, Pl.38; S. B. Downey, *Dura Final Rep.*, III, 1, 2, Los Angeles 1977, 9-11 no.2, Pl.I.2; photo Dura-Europos Publications, Yale University.

Plate XXXII

a) Hatra, Iraq, temple 'of Ba𝑐alshamin', relief of three goddesses and a bearded god, each wearing a *polos*; *c.* A.D.100-241; Ht.136 (= Mosul Museum, 40); Mosul marble, size 77 × 30 × 15; see *Mosul Museum Catalogue*, Baghdad 1958, 16; Safar, *Hatra*, 214, Pl.201; photo Dir. Ant., Baghdad.

b) Hatra, Iraq, sanctuary of the Sun, back wall of building A, frontal relief bust of a peplos-wearing goddess labelled Martên, between bearded snakes and acanthus leaves; second century A.D.; Hatra, Ht.444; limestone, size 65 × 125; see Al-Salihi, *Sculptures*, 124-126 no.51, fig.76; Safar, *Hatra*, 114, Pl.89; photo Dir. Ant., Baghdad.

Plate XXXIII

a) Palmyra, Syria, altar relief of Allat, named, seated in civil dress with lion; first century A.D.; Palmyra Museum 1887; limestone, height 68; see P. Collart, etc., *Le sanctuaire de Baalshamin*, Rome, I, 1969, 223, II, 1969, Pl.CVIII.3, III, 1971, no. 26; Drijvers, *Religion*, 18, Pl.XLV.1; Colledge, *Palmyra*, 53, Pl.49; photo P. Collart and the Swiss Archaeological Mission to Palmyra.

b) Khirbet es Sané, north-west of Palmyra, Syria, relief from shrine with a figure of Athena, addressed as Allat, before a worshipper; *c.* A.D.200-270; National Museum, Damascus, C.2351; limestone, size 57 × 50; see especially H. Seyrig, *Syria* 14, 1933, 14f., Pl.IV.1; J. Cantineau, *Syria* 14, 1933, 181, inscription 5; Schlumberger, *Palmyrène*, 78 no.1, Pl.XXXVII,1; T Borkowska, *Studia Palmyreńskie* 1, 1966, 110-111 no.19; H. Seyrig, *Syria* 47, 1970, 83, fig.5 = *AS* 89; Drijvers, *Religion*, 20, Pl.LVIII; Colledge, *Palmyra*, 49; photo InfA 916.

c) Hatra, Iraq, relief of a central Athena figure (Allat ?) and two other goddesses standing on a lion; *c.* A.D.100-241; Iraq Museum, Baghdad, IM 56774; limestone, size 118 × 72; see especially N. Al-Asil, *Illustrated London News*, December 25 1954, 1160, fig.2; H. J. Lenzen, *AA*, 1955, 346, fig.4; *Iraq Museum Catalogue*, Baghdad 1960, 199, Pl.53; D. Homes-Fredericq, *Hatra et ses sculptures parthes*, Istanbul 1963, 57 no.36; Al-Salihi, *Sculptures*, 109-111 no.42, fig.65; Safar, *Hatra*, 233, Pl.224; photo Dir. Ant., Baghdad.

Plate XXXIV

a) Hatra, Iraq, relief of an eagle before two religious standards; dated A.D.187; Iraq Museum, Baghdad, IM 58151; limestone, size 60 × 60 × 9; see *Iraq Museum Catalogue*, Baghdad 1960, 198, Pl.49; Safar, *Hatra*, 295, Pl.293; photo Dir. Ant., Baghdad.

b) Marzouga, north-west of Palmyra, Syria, relief of a lion dedicated to Baᶜalshamin; dated April, A.D.216; National Museum, Damascus, 9014; limestone size 28 × 39 × 6/9; see Schlumberger, *Palmyrène*, 84 no.7, 167 no. 61; T. Borkowska, *Studia Palmyreńskie* 1, 1966, 114 no.28; P. Collart, *Le sanctuaire de Baalshamin*, Rome 1969, I, 202, II, Pl.CIV.3; Drijvers, *Religion*, 14-15, Pl.XXVII; Colledge, *Palmyra*, 52, Pl.46; photo InfA p.24.

c) Palmyra, precinct of Bel, relief of a god (?) on a dromedary; *c.* A.D.50-250; National Museum, Damascus, 10943; limestone, height *c.* 70; see H. Seyrig, *Syria* 22, 1941, 33-34, Pl.I.2; M. Morehart, *Berytus* 12, 1956-57, 58 no.10, fig.10; J. Starcky, *Archeologia* 16, Paris 1967, 31, fig.2; Colledge, *Palmyra*, 43, Pl.33; photo InfA F618.

Plate XXXV

a) Assur, Iraq, Gate House, inscribed funerary relief showing a bearded man in profile; dated 89/88 B.C. or A.D.12/13 (?); Istanbul Archaeological Museum 1072/4736; limestone, height *c.* 2 m.; see W. Andrae and H. Lenzen, 'Die Partherstadt Assur', *WVDOG* 57, 1933, 106, Pl.59a, d; D. Schlumberger, *L'orient hellénisé*, Paris 1970, 120, fig.42; Colledge, *Parthian art*, 98, Pl.28a; photo Arkeoloji Müzeleri, Istanbul.

b) Palmyra, Syria, inscribed funerary relief busts of a bearded man holding a sword hilt (Group II Qc4) and his mourning mother with cup, disarrayed hair and bared breast with three parallel gashes shown in which remain traces of red paint (Group II Eb22*Bh*); *c.* A.D.150-175; American University Museum, Beirut, 33.12; limestone, size 43 × 61; see H. Ingholt, *Berytus* 1, 1934, 40-42, Pl.X.1; H. Seyrig, *AAS* 1, 1951, 33; S. Abdul Hak, *AAS* 2, 1952, 236-237; Colledge, *Palmyra* 63, 70, Pl.65; photo American University Museum, Beirut.

c) Palmyra, Syria, relief from the underground tomb (hypogeum) of Malkû showing a family at a funeral banquet; *c.* A.D.200-250; National Museum, Damascus, C.4947; limestone, size 192 × 201; see especially S. Abdul Hak, *Catalogue illustré du .. musée de Damas*, Damascus 1951, 46, Pl.XIX.2; A.F. Al-'Ush, *Catalogue du musée national de Damas*, Damascus 1969, 123 no. 1; D. Schlumberger, *L'orient hellénisé*, Paris 1970, 84, Pl.15; Colledge, *Palmyra*, 76, Pl.100; Colledge, *Parthian art*, 98, Pl.30b; photo Direction Générale des Antiquités, Damascus.

Plate XXXVI

Palmyra, Syria, Tomb of the Three Brothers, recess (exedra) painted with an animal dado, Victories on globes holding up medallion busts, and scenes of Achilles (rear lunette) and the rape of Ganymede (ceiling medallion); *c.* A.D.160-191 (?); in situ; powdered metallic oxide colours on smoothed plaster, total height *c.* 5 m.; see especially J. Strzygowski, *Orient oder Rom,* Leipzig 1901, 11ff., 24ff., figs.2-3, Pl.I; C. H. Kraeling, *AAS* 11-12, 1961-65, 13-18; Colledge, *Palmyra*, 84-87, Pls.115-117; photo Holle Bildarchiv, Baden-Baden (D. Schlumberger, *L'orient hellénisé*, Paris 1970).

Plate XXXVII

a) Kakzu, north Iraq, sarcophagus with relief decoration showing a nude (?) goddess in an aedicula; late Parthian period; Iraq Museum, Baghdad, IM 15418; blue-glazed terracotta, length *c.* 2 m.; see G. Furlani, *Iraq* 1, 1934, 90-91 no.262, Pl.XII; photo Colledge.

b) Uruk (Warka), south Iraq, sarcophagus with relief decoration of a 'nude soldier' in panels; late Parthian period; British Museum, London, 92006; green-glazed terracotta, length 195; see Ghirshman, *Iran*, Pl.131; Colledge, *Parthian art*, 110, Pl.43b; photo British Museum, courtesy of the Trustees.

Plate XXXVIII

a) Palmyra, Syria, beam relief from the temple of Bel representing a sanctuary with two gods, probably Malakbel (centre) and ʿAglibôl (right); *c.* A.D.32; sub situ; limestone, height *c.* 160; see especially H. Seyrig, *Syria* 15, 1934, 173-178, Pl.XXII = *AS* II no.17.4, 27-31; H. Seyrig, *Syria* 19, 1938, 304; D. Schlumberger, *L'orient hellénisé*, Paris 1970, 194, 196; J. Wais, *Studia Palmyreńskie* 4, 1970, 14, fig.10; H. Seyrig, *Syria* 48, 1971, 100f., cf.131; Drijvers, *Religion*, 10, Pl.IV.1; Colledge, *Palmyra*, 36, Pl.19; photo InfA.

b) Palmyra, Syria, beam relief from the temple of Bel representing a battle between a snake-legged giant (left) and deities, possibly identifiable (from left) as a horse-rider - Shadrafa - Artemis (i.e. Atargatis, or Nanai ?) - Poseidon (Elqônerâ ?) - Arṣû (?) - Heracles (Nergal ?); c. A.D.32; sub situ; limestone, total height c. 3 m.; see especially H. Seyrig, *Syria* 15, 1934, 165-173, Pls.XX, XXIV.1 = *AS* II no.17.3, 20-27; H. Seyrig, *Syria* 18, 1937, 37-38 = *AS* 21.3; J. Starcky, *Syria* 26, 1949, 72-73, fig.8; D. Schlumberger, *L'orient hellénisé*, Paris 1970, 85, 89; Drijvers, *Religion*, 10, Pl.IV.2; Colledge, *Palmyra*, 36, fig.15; Colledge, *Parthian art*, 96; photo InfA.

c) Palmyra, Syria, niche lintel relief from the sanctuary of Baᶜalshamin with a central eagle (symbolizing Baᶜalshamin ?), other eagles, rosettes and the busts of gods, probably ᶜAglibôl (left of centre) and Malakbel; (mid-?) first century A.D.; Palmyra Museum B.1906/6850; limestone, size 84 × 264 × 24; see especially D. Schlumberger, *Syria* 37, 1960, 266-268, Pl.XI.1; P. Collart etc., *Le sanctuaire de Baalshamin*, Rome 1969, I, 162-164, 173-175, 209-227, II, Pl.XCVII.1-3; J. Wais, *Studia Palmyreńskie* 4, 1970, 46 fig.40; Drijvers, *Religion*, 16, Pl.XXXII; Colledge, *Palmyra*, 33, Pl.12; photo P. Collart and the Swiss Archaeological Mission to Palmyra.

Plate XXXIX

a) Dura-Europos, east Syria, wall-painting on the south wall of the *naos* of the temple of Bel depicting priests (in conical headdresses) and the family of Konon sacrificing; c. A.D.180 (?); National Museum, Damascus; metalllic oxide paints on smoothed plaster, height c. 2.5 m.; see F. Cumont, *Fouilles de Doura-Europos*, Paris 1926, 58-64, Pls. XXXI-XLI; A Perkins, *The art of Dura-Europos*, Oxford 1973, 38-41, Pl.10; Drijvers, *Religion*, 22, Pl.LXXX; Colledge, *Parthian art*, 119, Pl.48c; photo Cumont, Pl.XXXI.

b) Palmyra, Syria, beam relief from the temple of Bel representing a religious procession involving a dromedary carrying a pavilion, a cameleer, a horse or donkey, and onlookers including two groups of wholly veiled women; c. A.D.32; sub situ; limestone with traces of paint, size c. 2 × 3 m.; see especially H. Seyrig, *Syria* 15, 1934, 159-165, Pl.XIX = *AS* II no.17.2, 14-20; R. De Vaux, *Revue Biblique* 44, 1935, 397-412, Pl.XV; P. Dussaud, *La pénétration des arabes*, Paris 1930, 113ff.; J. Pirenne, *Syria* 38, 1961, 292, fig.3b; H. Seyrig, *Syria* 47, 1970, 91; D. Schlumberger, *Syria* 48, 1971, 129-131; M. Gawlikowski, *Le temple palmyrénien*, Warsaw 1973, 26-48; Drijvers, *Religion*, 11, Pl.V; Colledge, *Palmyra*, 37, Pl.20; photo Colledge.

c) Palmyra, Syria, altar dedicated 'to him whose name is blessed for ever' with relief of two figures with hands raised in prayer; c. A.D.200-270; Ny Carlsberg Glyptotek, Copenhagen, 1080; limestone, size 46 × 20; see D. Simonsen, *Sculpture et inscriptions de Palmyre*, Copenhagen 1889, 45 no. El, Pl.XIV; J. B. Chabot, *Choix d'inscriptions de Palmyre*, Paris 1922, 79, 86, Pl.XXIII.4; photo Ny Carlsberg Glyptotek.

Plate XL

a) Nihavand, west Iran, figurine representing Zeus; third or second century B.C. (?); Teheran Museum; bronze, height c. 13; see Ghirshman, *Iran*, 18, Pl.23E; M. A. R. Colledge, *The Parthians*, London 1967, Pl.28c; photo Service Photographique, Muzeh-e Iran-e Bastan, Teheran.

b) Hatra, Iraq, disc portraying deities, possibly (from left) Heracles - Zeus - Hera -Poseidon; *c.* A.D.100-241; Iraq Museum, Baghdad, IM 56704; ivory, diameter *c.* 9; see N. Al-Asil, *Illustrated London News*, December 25, 1954, 1161, fig.7; S. B. Downey, *Berytus* 16, 1966, 101; Safar, *Hatra*, 246, Pl.236; Colledge, *Parthian art*, 101, Pl.45a; photo Dir. Ant., Baghdad.

Plate XLI

a) Old Nisa, Turkmenistan, U.S.S.R., 'metopes' from the 'Round Hall' with designs in relief including a club and lion-head; third or second centuries B.C. (?); terracotta, size *c.* 40 × 40; see especially M. E. Masson and G. A. Pugachenkova, *Trudi IUTAKE* 1, 1949, 217; G. A. Pugachenkova, *VDI*, 1951 (4), 191-4, fig.2; G. A. Pugachenkova, *Trudi IUTAKE* 6, 1958, 97, 102; G. A. Koshelenko, *Kultura Parfii*, Moscow 1966, 32; G. A. Pugachenkova, *Iskusstvo Turkmenistana*, Moscow 1967, Pl.15; Colledge, *Parthian art*, 97, fig.41; drawing from Pugachenkova, 1958, 97.

b) Bisutun (Behistun), west Iran, inscribed rock relief of Heracles reclining ('Hercules cubans') with cup, club, bow and quiver, above an earlier lion; dated June, 148 B.C.; in situ; size *c.* 190 × 210; see especial R. N. Frye, *The heritage of Persia*, London 1962, 150, figs.69-70; L. Robert, *Gnomon* 35, 1963, 76 (Greek inscription); S. B. Downey, *Dura Final Rep.*, I, 1, 1, 1, Pl.I.1-2; W. Kleiss, *AMI n.f.* 3, 1970, 145, Pl.66; A. D. H. Bivar, *JRAS* 1970, 132; Colledge, *Parthian art*, 90, fig. 39A; drawing Kleiss, 1970, fig. 11.

c) Hatra, Iraq, shrine VII, 'cult bank' with relief of Heracles in three stages of fighting a Centaur ('continuous narrative') above a grape and leaf spiral; *c.* A.D.100-241; Iraq Museum, Baghdad, IM 58088; Mosul marble, size 62 × 32; see S. B. Downey, *Berytus* 16, 1966, 101-106, Pl.XVI; Safar, *Hatra*, 264, Pl.290; photo Dir. Ant., Baghdad.

Plate XLII

a) Palmyra, Syria, Roman camp area, locally executed relief with Latin inscription portraying Leto with palm branch and ball of wool wearing local costume, and a nude Apollo; *c.* A.D.150-175; Palmyra Museum; limestone, size 58 × 65; see H. Seyrig, *Syria* 14, 1933, 162-164, Pl.XXI.1 = *AS* I no.12, 80-82; T. Borkowska, *Studia Palmyreńskie* 1, 1966, 113 no.26, fig.8; J. T. Milik, *Dédicaces faites par des dieux*, Paris 1972, 164; Drijvers, *Religion*, 19, Pl.LII.1; Colledge, *Palmyra*, 48, 225, Pl.40; photo InfA F626.

b) Surkh Kotal, Afghanistan, section of architectural frieze with garlands carried by Erotes in relief; second century A.D.; Kabul Museum; limestone, height *c.* 1 m.; see D. Schlumberger, *L'orient hellénisé*, Paris 1970, 62, Pl.12; Photo DAFA.

c) Kuh-i Khwaja, east Iran, wall-painting once in the north 'gallery' of the building complex depicting three standing gods, one with the trident of Poseidon (here, of the Indian Śiva ?) and one with a winged helmet like Hermes' (here, of Iranian Verethraghna ?); first to third centuries A.D.; metallic oxide paints on smoothed plaster; see E. Herzfeld, *Archaeological history of Iran*, Oxford 1935, 66-75, Pl.CIV; Ghirshman, *Iran*, 42, Pl.57; G. Gullini, *Architettura iranica*, Turin 1964, 443-453; D. Schlumberger, *L'orient hellénisé*, Paris 1970, 54, 60; Colledge, *Parthian art*, 119, Pl.48b; photo Herzfeld, 1935, courtesy of Mrs. C. M. Bradford.

Plate XLIII

a) Old Nisa, Turkmenistan, U.S.S.R., 'Treasury', rhytons carved with anthropomorphic and animal protomai, and friezes of Olympian deities, sacrifices, animals and heads; second century B.C. (?); Leningrad, Hermitage Museum; ivory, height *c.* 20; see especially M. E. Masson and G. A. Pugachenkova, *Trudi IUTAKE* IV.1, Ashkhabad 1959, IV.2, Moscow 1956; Ghirshman, *Iran*, 30, fig.41; G. A. Pugachenkova, *Iskusstvo Turkmenistana*, Moscow 1967, fig.12, Pls.27-37; G. Frumkin, *Archaeology in Soviet Central Asia*, Leiden 1970, 149-150, Pls.LXI-LXVII; D. Schlumberger, *L'orient hellénisé*, Paris 1970, 36, Pls.7, 8; Colledge, *Parthian art*, 116, Pl.37; photo *Union Soviétique*, 1954.

b) Nineveh, Iraq, shrine, statue of a 'Hermes' figure; first to earlier third centuries A.D. (?); Iraq Museum, Baghdad, IM 59094; limestone, height *c.* 160; see M. A. Mustafa, *Sumer* 10, 1954, 281-283, figs.; Colledge, *Parthian art*, 84, Pl.5; photo Dir. Ant., Baghdad.

c) Denavar, west Iran, fragment of a bowl or altar with heads of Satyrs and Sileni; *c.* 300-150 B.C. (?); Teheran Museum 2402; limestone, height 33; see Ghirshman, *Iran*, 18, Pls.21-22; D. Schlumberger, *L'orient hellénisé*, Paris 1970, 31; Colledge, *Parthian art*, 114, Pl.31a; cf. B. Rowland, *Art Quarterly* 18, 1955, 171-174; photo Muzeh-e Iran-e Bastan, Teheran.

Plate XLIV

a) Palmyra, Syria, ceiling of the north recess (thalamos) in the temple of Bel with reliefs depicting the busts of the planetary deities Bel (?)/Zeus/Jupiter (centre), Ares/Mars (above him), and (anticlockwise) the sun, Hermes/Mercury, Saturn, Aphrodite/Venus with veil, and the moon, with the zodiac and eagles around; *c.* A.D.32; in situ; limestone, width *c.* 3 m.; see H. Seyrig, *Syria* 14, 1933, 258-260, fig.5, corrected *AS* IV no.14, frontispiece; J. Wais, *Studia Palmyreńskie* 4, 1970, 31-32, fig.26; cf. H. Seyrig, *Syria* 48, 1971, 85-114; P. Brykczyński, *Studia Palmyreńskie* 6, 1975, 52-68, figs.1,2; Drijvers, *Religion*, 9, Pl.II; Colledge, *Palmyra*, 38-39, fig.18, Pl.21; photo InfA 241.

b) Hatra, Iraq, shrine V, inscribed lintel relief showing the reclining (king ?) WLGŠ (?) (of Hatra ?) between figures and winged personified Victories holding wreaths; (mid ?) second century A.D.; Iraq Museum, Baghdad, IM 56751; limestone, size 58 × 267; see especially N. Al-Asil, *Illustrated London News*, December 18, 1954, 1116, fig.9; S. B. Downey, *Berytus* 16, 1966, 106; Al-Salihi, *Sculptures*, 143; J. T. Milik, *Dédicaces faites par des dieux*, Paris 1972, 363-364; Safar, *Hatra*, 247, Pl.23; Colledge, *Parthian art*, 93, Pl.23; photo Dir. Ant., Baghdad.

c) Palmyra, Syria, Tomb of the Three Brothers, painting of the Evil Eye in the painted recess (exedra); see above, Pl.XXXVI; drawing after J. B. Chabot, *Choix d'inscriptions de Palmyre*, Paris 1922, Pl.XVI.3.

Plate XLV

a) Edessa (Urfa), south Turkey, cave-tomb in the necropolis, inscribed funerary mosaic depicting a phoenix between two trees, standing on a wreathed sacred pillar above a sarcophagus, probably symbolizing rebirth; dated A.D.235/6; in situ; coloured cut stone cubes (tesserae) in lime mortar, height *c.* 2 m.; see J. B. Segal, *Archaeology* 12 (3), autumn 1959, 155, fig.; J. B. Segal, *Edessa, the Blessed City*, Oxford 1970, 33, 56, Pl.43; Colledge, *Parthian art*, 118, Pl.47b; photo J. B. Segal, 1970, Pl.43.

b) Palmyra, Syria, temple of Bel, underside (soffit) of beam with floral spiral containing Eros, Victory and other figures ('inhabited scroll'); *c.* A.D.32; sub situ; limestone, height *c.* 1 m.; see H. Seyrig, *Syria* 15, 1934, 184, Pl.XXI.3 = *AS* II no.17, 59; J. M. C. Toynbee, *Papers of the British School at Athens* 18, 1950, 32; M. Wegner, *Ornamente kaiserliche Bauten Roms*, Cologne 1957, 9-11, Pl.3a; B. Filarska, *Studia Palmyreńskie* 2, 1967, 16, fig.14; Colledge, *Palmyra*, 38, Pl.18; cf. above, Pl.I; photo InfA B.8.

c) Found in Tibet (originally from Bactria ?), bowl with figures, a libation (?) scene (at top) and trees in repoussé; *c.* 250 B.C. - A.D.100 (?); private collection; silver, diameter 21; see P. Denwood, *Iran* 11, 1973, 121-127, Pls.I-IV; Colledge, *Parthian art*, 115, 124, Pl.46b; photo Ashmolean Museum, Oxford, courtesy Dr. D. L. Snellgrove.

Plate XLVI

a) Bîmarân, near Jelâlâbâd, Afghanistan, Buddhist reliquary, with reliefs of the Buddha flanked by the gods Indra and Brahma, in repoussé; *c.* A.D.130-225 (?); British Museum, London; gold inlaid with rubies, height 7; see B. Rowland, *The art and architecture of India*, London 1952, 78-79, Pl.38B; T. Talbot Rice, *Ancient arts of central Asia*, London 1965, 144-145, Pl.129; Colledge, *Parthian art*, 115, Pl.36; photo British Museum, courtesy of the Trustees.

b) Gandhara, west Pakistan, architectural relief with men (nobles, or donors ?) in Iranian (Kushan ?) dress; second or third century A.D.; Royal Ontario Museum, Toronto, 939.17.19; dark grey schist, size 23.6 × 50.8; see Ghirshman, *Iran*, 3, fig.5; R. E. M. Wheeler, *Flames over Persepolis*, London 1968, 146-147; photo Royal Ontario Museum, negative 64FAE18.

c) Takht-i Bahî, Gandhara, west Pakistan, architectural relief with Buddhist scene, perhaps the 'Presentation of the bride to Siddhârta'; probably second or earlier third century A.D.; British Museum, London; schist, height 14; see J. H. Marshall, *The Buddhist art of Gandhara*, Cambridge 1960, 34, fig.41; M. Hallade, *Gandharan art of north India*, New York 1968, Pl.4; Colledge, *Parthian art*, 94, Pl.24b; photo British Museum, courtesy of the Trustees.

Plate XLVII

a) Hatra, Iraq, temple C, locally executed head perhaps representing the Roman emperor Trajan (reigned A.D.98-117); *c.* A.D.100-241; Iraq Museum, Baghdad, IM 73039; Mosul marble, size 27 × 21.7; see J. M. C. Toynbee, *Sumer* 26, 1970, 231-235,

Pls.1-2; J. M. C. Toynbee, *Journal of Roman Studies* 62, 1972, 106-107, Pl.V; Safar, *Hatra*, 103, Pl.71; photo Dir. Ant., Baghdad.

b) Dura-Euopos, east Syria, Mithraeum, larger inscribed relief of the god Mithras slaying the bull, with the dedicant's family, three divine busts and the zodiac; dated A.D.170/1; Yale University Art Gallery 1935.98; gypsum, size 76 × 106 × 10/11; see L. A. Campbell, etc., *Dura Prelim. Rep.* VII/VIII, New Haven 1939, 84, 95ff., Pls.XXIX.2, XXX; A. Perkins, *The art of Dura-Europos*, Oxford 1973, 86-88, Pl.35; F. Cumont, in: J. R. Hinnells, ed., *Proceedings of the First International Congress of Mithraic Studies*, Manchester 1975, 166-169; S. B. Downey, *Dura Final Rep.*, III, 1, 2, Los Angeles 1977, 25-29 no.8, Pl.IV.8; photo Yale University Art Gallery, Dura-Europos Publications.

c) Dura-Europos, east Syria, Christian Baptistry, wall-painting behind the font of a beardless Christ as the Good Shepherd, with Adam and Eve (bottom left) added afterwards; towards A.D.250; Yale University Art Gallery; metallic oxide paints on smoothed plaster, height *c.* 2 m.; see C. H. Kraeling, *Dura Final Rep.*, VIII, 2, New Haven 1967, 45-88; A. Perkins, *The art of Dura-Europos*, Oxford 1973, 52-55, Pls.17-18; Colledge, *Parthian art*, 120, Pl.48d; photo Yale University Art Gallery, Dura-Europos Publications.

Plate XLVIII

Dura-Europos, east Syria, Synagogue, north-west section with the Torah Shrine and wall-paintings depicting episodes from the Old Testament; *c.* A.D.244/5; Damascus Museum; metallic oxide paints on smoothed plaster, height *c.* 5 m.; see especially C. H. Kraeling, *Dura Final Rep.*, VIII, 1, New Haven, 1956, 34-354; J. Gutmann, ed., *The Dura-Europos Synagogue: a re-evaluation (1932-1972)*, Montana 1973; A. Perkins, *The art of Dura-Europos*, Oxford 1973, 55-65, Pls.19-24; Colledge, *Parthian art*, 120-121, Pl.49; photo Yale University Art Gallery, Dura-Europos Publications.

PLATES I-XLVIII

Palmyra, air view from south-east

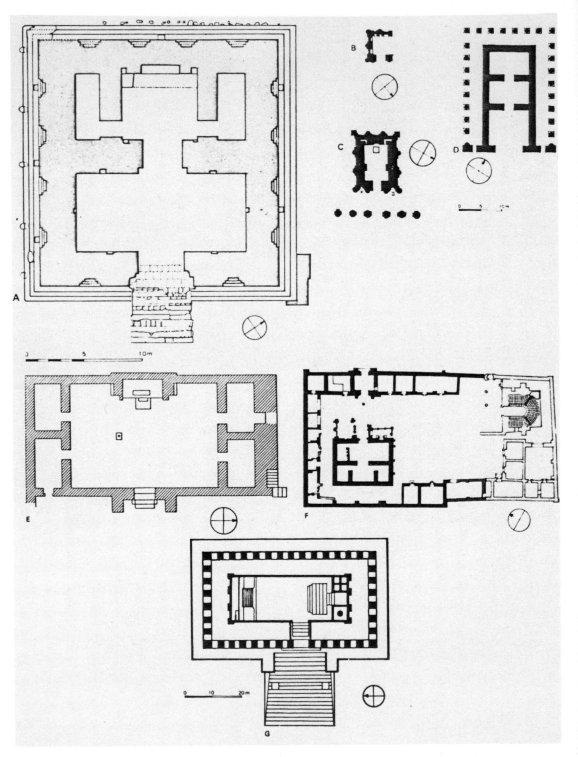

Plan of 'broad room' temples

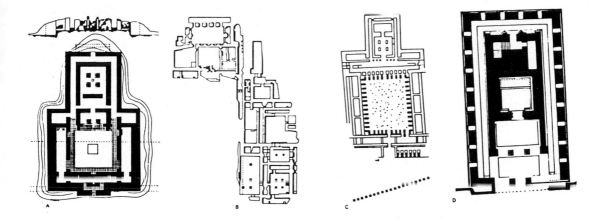

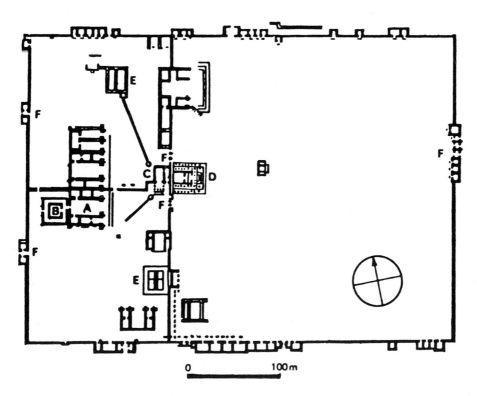

Plans of 'centralized square' and iwan temples

a) Khurna, Iran

b) Old Nisa, 'Square Hall', reconstruction of interior

c) Hatra, Iraq, iwans of Sun sanctuary

a) Temple of Bel, *c.* A.D. 32, from south-east

b) Tomb-tower of Elahbel, A.D. 103

c) Hypogeum of Iarhai, *c.* A.D. 200-270

Plate VI   *Zeus-Oromasdes*

a) Nemrud Dağ, Commagene, colossal head, *c.* 69-31 B.C.

b) Nemrud Dağ, Commagene, handshake relief, *c.* 69-31 B.C.

c) Nemrud Dağ, Commagene, hierothesion east terrace, *c.* 69-31 B.C.

a) Nemrud Dağ, Commagene, colossal head,
c. 69-31 B.C.

b) Nemrud Dağ, Commagene, handshake
relief, *c.* 69-31 B.C.

c) Bard-i Nishandeh, Iran, capital relief,
second century A.D.?

Plate VIII   *Verethraghna*

a) Nemrud Dağ, Commagene, colossal head, *c.* 69-31 B.C.

b) Arsameia on the Nymphaios, Commagene, handshake relief, *c.* 69-31 B.C.

c) Tang-i Butan, Iran, rock relief, *c.* A.D. 100-200?

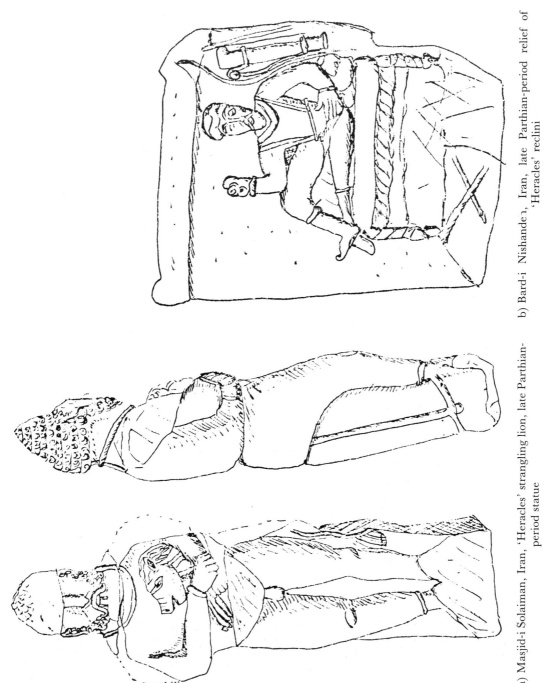

a) Masjid-i Solaiman, Iran, 'Heracles' strangling lion, late Parthian-period statue

b) Bard-i Nishandeɪn, Iran, late Parthian-period relief of 'Heracles' reclini

Plate X   *Anahita, baetyl*

a) Bard-i Nishandeh, Iran, late Parthian-period capital with Anahita (?) in relief

b) Iran, late Parthian-period figurine of Anahita (?)

c) Tang-i Sarvak, Elymais, Iran, late Parthian-period rock relief including a baetyl (?)

b) Tang-i Sarvak, Elymais, Iran, late Parthian-period rock relief of figure wrestling with a lion

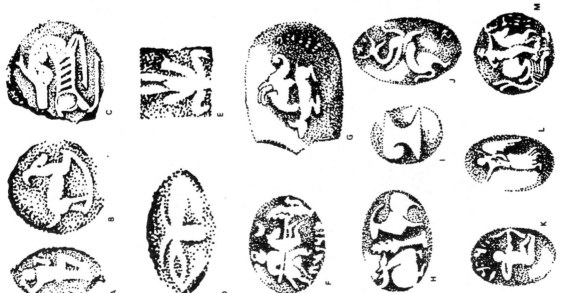

a) Seal-impressions

Plate XII   *Iranian investiture reliefs*

a) Nemrud Dağ, Commagene, fragment of investiture relief, *c.* 69-31 B.C.

b) Nemrud Dağ, Commagene, lion-horoscope relief, 7 July, 62 B.C.

c) Tang-i Sarvak, Elymais, Iran, late Parthian-period reliefs on second rock, face b

b) Bisutun, Iran, adjacent rock reliefs of Mithradates II (left) and Gotarzes

a) Bard-i Nishandeh, Iran, late Parthian-
period relief of king sacrificing

c) Tang-i Sarvak, Elymais, Iran, late Parthian-period reliefs
on the second rock, face

Plate XIV   *Iranian dynastic groups*

a) Khaltchayan, north Bactria, mid-Parthian wall reliefs of (A) royalty, (B) nobles with a chariot goddess and (C) mounted archers.

b) Kuh-i Khwaja, east Iran, wall-painting of king and queen, first to third centuries A.D.

a) Nemrud Dağ, Commagene, relief of Xerxes I, *c.* 69-31 B.C.

b) Shami, Iran, bronze chieftain statue, *c.* 50 B.C.- A.D. 150

c) Surkh Kotal, Afghanistan, statue of Kushan prince, *c.* A.D. 130

d) Mathura, north India, statue of king Vima Kaphises, *c.* A.D. 130

Plate XVI   *Persian, Seleucid and Parthian coins*

First line, for "tt" read "rr".

Plate XVIII   *Iranian royal relief*

a) Hung-i Nauruzi, Elymais, Iran, rock relief of mounted king, *c.* 50 B.C. - A.D. 50

b) Bisutun, Iran, sketch of rock relief of Mithradates II, *c.* 123-110 B.C.?

c) Susa, Iran, relief of Artabanus V and Khwasak, A.D. 215

Plate XX   *The triad of Bel at Palmyra, Syria*

a) Relief of (from left) Malakbel - Baᶜalshamîn - Bel - ᶜAglibôl - Astarte (named),
c. A.D. 100-150

b) Relief perhaps of (from left) Iarḥibôl - Bel - ᶜAglibôl -
Arṣû, first or second century A.D.

c) Relief of (from left) Arṣû - Iarḥibôl - Bel - ᶜAglibôl
(named), *c.* A.D. 100

a) Relief of (from left) worshipper - Astarte - ᶜAglibôl - Malakbel - Bel - Baᶜalshamîn — Nemesis - Arṣû (named), A.D. 152

b) Pedimented relief of (from left) goddess - Iarḥibôl (?) - Bel (?) - ᶜAglibôl (named), A.D. 119 (?)

Plate XXII   *Dura-Europos, Syria, temple of Bel*

Wall-painting of Otes casting incense before five deities, around A.D. 200

Wall-painting of tribune Terentius sacrificing before three gods above the named Tychai (Fortunes) of Dura-Europos (to our right) and Palmyra, *c.* A.D. 239

Plate XXIV   *Ba^calshamîn, Nebû*

a) Relief from Dura-Europos, east Syria, of dedicant before the seated, named god Zeus Kyrios/Ba^calshamîn, A.D. 31

c) Dura-Europos, east Syria, statuette of Nebû (named), *c.* A.D. 50-250

b) Relief from Palmyra (?), Syria, perhaps of (from left) ^cAglibôl (?) - Ba^calshamîn (?) - Malakbel (?), first century A.D.

a) Palmyra, Syria, relief perhaps of (from left) 'Heracles'/Nergal (?) - goddess - ʿAglibôl - Malakbel (?), first century A.D. (?)

b) Hatra, Iraq, shrine V, statuette of 'Heracles'/Nergal (?), *c.* A.D. 100-241

c) Hatra, Iraq, shrine VIII, statuette of radiate god, *c.* A.D. 100-241

Plate XXVI   Marên

b) Hatra, Iraq, shrine I, relief bust of radiate god. c. A.D. 100-241

a) Hatra, Iraq, Sun sanctuary, Building A, relief bust of god named

a) Palmyra, Syria, named relief of Shadrafa,
A.D. 55

b) Dura-Europos, east Syria, relief of worshipper
before named cuirassed god Aphlad, *c.* A.D. 54

c) Palmyra, Syria, two-tier relief with busts of a god in civil dress and in cuirass (Malakbel ?)
and eagles, first century A.D.

Plate XXVIII

b) Near Palmyra, Syria, relief of horse-riding gods named Abgal and Ashar, A.D. 154

a) Dura-Europos, east Syria, relief of gods named Asherū and Saʿad, *c.* A.D. 50-250

c) Near Palmyra, Syria, relief of three gods before two worshippers (on left) dedicated to mlk? A.D. 263

a) Dura-Europos, east Syria, inscribed relief of the Gad (Fortune) of Dura-Europos
(centre), A.D. 159

b) Dura-Europos, east Syria, inscribed relief of the Gad (Fortune) of Palmyra
(centre), A.D. 159

Plate XXX   *Bar-Marên and 'Aššur-Bel' (Apollo of Hierapolis?)*

a) Hatra, Iraq, Sun sanctuary, building A, relief bust of god named Bar-Marên, second century A.D.

c) Hatra, Iraq, shrine V, statue of god (Aššur-Bel, or Apollo of Hierapolis ?), *c.* A.D. 100-241

b) Hatra, Iraq, Sun sanctuary, bronze Dionysus mask inscribed '...for Bar-Marên', *c.* A.D. 100-241

a) Hatra, Iraq, shrine I, relief of god, goddess and religious standards, *c.* A.D. 100-241

b) Dura-Europos, east Syria, temple of Atargatis, relief of goddess, god and religious standard, *c.* A.D. 50-250

a) Hatra, Iraq, temple 'of Baʿalshamîn', relief of three goddesses and god in *polos*, *c.* A.D. 100-241

b) Hatra, Iraq, Sun sanctuary, building A, relief bust of goddess named Martên, second century A.D.

a) Palmyra, Syria, altar relief of Allat, named, first century A.D.

b) Near Palmyra, Syria, relief of worshipper before Allat (named), *c.* A.D. 200-270

c) Hatra, Iraq, relief with Athena figure (Allat?) between two other goddesses on lion, *c.* A.D. 100-241

a) Hatra, Iraq, relief of eagle before two religious standards, A.D. 187

b) Near Palmyra, Syria, relief of lion dedicated to
Baᶜalshamîn, A.D. 216

c) Palmyra; Syria, Bel precinct, relief of
(divine ?) dromedary rider, *c.* A.D. 50-250

a) Aššur, Iraq, Gate house, inscribed funerary relief of man, 89/88 B.C. or A.D. 12/13 (?)

b) Palmyra, Syria, funerary relief busts of man and mourning mother, *c.* A.D. 150-175

c) Palmyra, Syria, hypogeum of Malkû, funerary banquet relief, *c.* A.D. 200-250

Plate XXXVI　　　　　　　*Funerary wall-painting*

Palmyra, Syria, painted exedra in the Tomb of the Three Brothers, *c.* A.D. 160-191 (?)

a) Kakzu, north Iraq, late Parthian-period sarcophagus with nude (?) goddess decoration

b) Uruk (Warka), south Iraq, late Parthian-period sarcophagus with 'nude soldier' panels

Plate XXXVIII   *Palmyra, Syria, temple reliefs*

a) Palmyra, Syria, Bel temple beam relief of a sanctuary with attendant (left), Malakbel centre) and
ᶜAglibôl (?), *c.* A.D. 32

b) Palmyra, Syria, Bel temple beam relief of a battle between a giant (left) and deities, *c.* A.D. 32

c) Palmyra, Syria, Baᶜalshamîn sanctuary, niche lintel with eagles and busts of ᶜAglibôl (?-left) and
Malakbel (?), (mid-?) first century A.D.

a) Dura-Europos, east Syria, temple of Bel, wall-painting of sacrifice, *c.* A.D. 100 (?)

b) Palmyra, Syria, Bel temple beam relief of a religious procession, *c.* A.D. 32

c) Palmyra, Syria, altar with relief of two figures praying, *c.* A.D. 200-270

Plate XL   *Zeus*

b) Hatra, Iraq, relief perhaps of (from left) Heracles - Zeus - Hera - Poseidon,

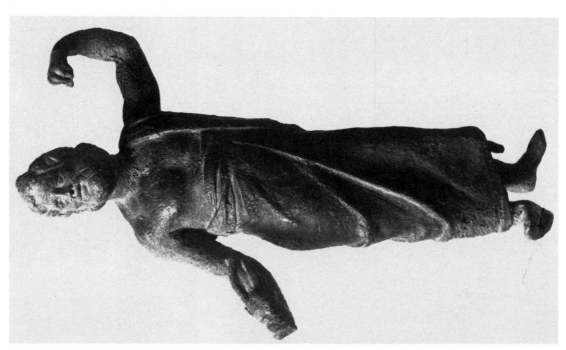

a) Nihavand, west Iran, figurine of Zeus, third or second century

c) Hatra, Iraq, shrine VII, 'cult bank' with relief of Heracles fighting a Centaur, *c.* A.D. 100-241

a) Old Nisa, U.S.S.R., early Parthian-period 'metopes' from Round Hall' with reliefs of lyre, club and lion-head

b) Bisutun, west Iran, inscribed, rock relief of Heracles reclining, 148 B.C.

Plate XLII   *Apollo, Leto, Eros, Poseidon (?)*

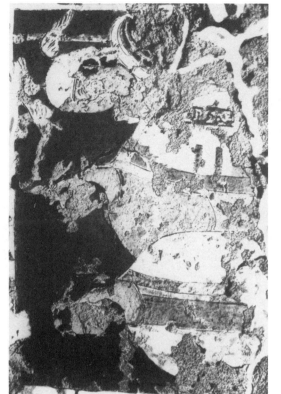

c) Kuh-i Khwaja, east Iran, wall-painting of three gods including Poseidon/Śiva (?) and Hermes/Verethraghna (?), first to third centuries A.D.

a) Palmyra, Syria, inscribed relief of Apollo and Leto, *c.* A.D. 150-175

c) Denavar, west Iran, fragmentary Silenus relief, *c.* 300-150 B.C. (?)

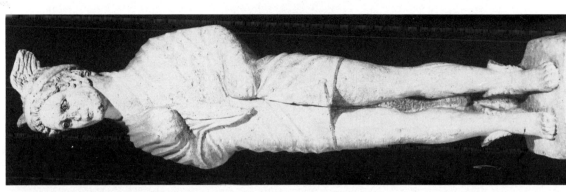

b) Nineveh, Iraq, shrine, Hermes-like statue, later Parthian period (?)

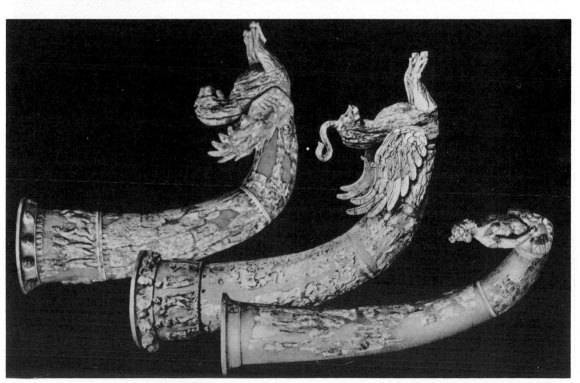

a) Old Nisa, U.S.S.R., 'Treasury', ivory rhytons with friezes of Olympian deities and (at top) Erotes, second century B.C. (?)

Plate XLIV   *Greek and Roman themes*

a) Palmyra, Syria, Bel temple north thalamos ceiling with reliefs of planetary busts and zodiac,
c. A.D. 32

b) Hatra, Iraq, shrine V, inscribed lintel relief of the reclining WLGŠ (?) and Victories, (mid-?) second
century A.D.

c) Palmyra, Syria, Tomb of the Three
Brothers, wall-painting of the Evil Eye,
c. A.D. 360-370 (?)

b) Palmyra, Syria, Bel temple beam underside relief of 'inhabitad scroll', *c.* A.D. 32

c) Bactria (? - found in Tibet), silver bowl with figures and (at top) libation scene, *c.* 250 B.C. - A.D. 100 (?)

a) Edessa, Turkey, cave-tomb funerary mosaic of phoenix above sarcophagus, A.D. 235/6

Plate XLVI *Indian religions*

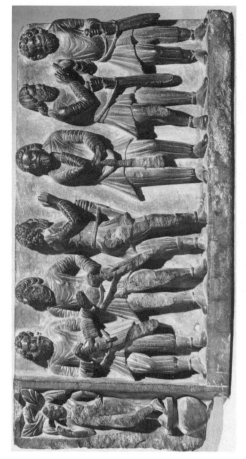

b) Gandhara, Pakistan, architectural relief with men in Iranian costume, second or third century A.D.

c) Takht-i Bahī, Pakistan, Buddhist relief perhaps of the 'Presentation of the bride to Siddhārta', second or earlier third century A.D.

a) Bīmarān, Afghanistan, Buddhist reliquary with the Buddha flanked by Indra and Brahma, *c.* A.D. 130-225 (?)

a) Hatra, Iraq, temple C, head (of Trajan ?), *c.* A.D. 100-241

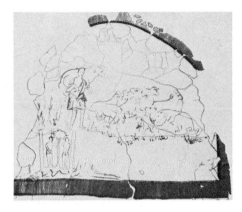

c) Dura-Europos, Syria, Christian Baptistry, wall-painting of Christ and Adam and Eve towards A.D. 250

b) Dura-Europos, Syria, Mithraeum, relief of Mithras slaying the bull and zodiac, A.D. 170/1

Plate XLVIII　　　　　　　　　*Judaism*

Dura-Europos, Syria, Synagogue, north-west part with Torah Shrine and wall-paintings of Old Testament scenes, *c.* A,D, 244/5